Inspiring Student Writers

Strategies and Examples for Teachers

a volume in
Literacy, Language, and Learning

Series Editor:
Patricia Ruggiano Schmidt,
Le Moyne College

Literacy, Language, and Learning

Patricia Ruggiano Schmidt, Series Editor

Inspiring
Student
Writers

Strategies and Examples for Teachers

edited by

Tom Scheft
North Carolina Central University

Information Age Publishing, Inc.
Charlotte, North Carolina • www.infoagepub.com

Library of Congress Cataloging-in-Publication Data

Inspiring student writers : strategies and examples for teachers / edited by Tom Scheft.
    p. cm. — (Language, literacy, and learning)
    Includes bibliographical references.
    ISBN 978-1-60752-037-5 (paperback) — ISBN 978-1-60752-038-2 (hardcover)
1. English language—Composition and exercises—Study and teaching.
2. Creative writing—Study and teaching. 3. English teachers. I. Scheft, Tom.

    LB1576.I868 2009
    808'.042071—dc22

                              2008051154

Printed in the United States of America.

To Daniel

To my parents

To my brothers and sisters

CONTENTS

APPENDIX

ACKNOWLEDGMENTS

I want to thank the people who helped me with this book directly and indirectly.

My son, Daniel—a never-ending source of humor, pride, and inspiration. He is the best—smart, funny, sensitive, and a blast to be around.

My parents, Bill and Gitty Scheft. Thank you for so many, many things—tangible and intangible.

Apart from the basics my mother taught me, she nurtured in me a desire to make things better—be they in my life or the lives of those around me. Anything I learned later from studying Martin Luther King, Jr. or Gandhi or Gloria Steinem or Malcolm X or Mr. Rogers, I first learned from my mother. She pointed me in the direction of teaching, a career I love.

My Dad was a fairly quiet role model who lived by rather basic values. He was a noncomplaining hard worker, a corporate leader who rolled up his sleeves along with everybody else, a team player who chose to give opportunities to many—especially his children.

My sisters—Andrea, Sally, and Harriet. My brothers—Bill and John. I am the oldest of six children. While we are different individuals, we share certain, distinct qualities. The Scheft kids are very motivated, very hardworking, funny, clever, nice people.

Sterling Hennis. Dr. Hennis taught the methods course in English-Education before I did my student teaching. Of the many great classroom teachers I've had, he is my favorite and the most inspirational. He was a visionary who encouraged his students to be visionaries. He showed us that the world was a boundless source of educational materials and experiences. Over the years he encouraged me to create with film and words.

Clyde Edgerton—a gifted writer, a great friend, and a helpful editor.

Andrew "Mac" Secrest. Mac is an award-winning journalist and civil rights activist who provided tremendous editing help with this book. As my brother Bill would say, Mac's fingerprints are all over this work. He helped me greatly—not only by pointing out certain errors and problems, but also by pushing me to rewrite and expand sections. As much as I didn't want to do some things, I realized Mac was right.

Here's an affectionate nod to all the wonderful colleagues and students I've worked with over the years.

And here's a heartfelt thanks to wonderful friends (Kris, John, Vicki, Jim, David, Pamela, Mark, Tony, Bob, Charlie, Rich, Erik, Isabel, Sue, Tommy, Kelly, Sof, Callie, Perry, Jonathan, Hagai, Ella, Jeff, Kevin, Ali, Laurie, Adrianne, Anita, Jim C., Leslie, Sandy, Elwood, Carol, Tom E., Patty S., Tim).

FOREWORD

Clyde Edgerton

Growing up, I wanted to be a cowboy or fireman, then doctor, then pilot. My mother wanted me to be a missionary or concert pianist, and my father, it seems, hoped I might be a banker.

I came to love stories and ideas—and talking about both—and so about the time I started college, I decided that if I could be a high school English teacher—stand in front of a classroom and be instrumental in freeing up ideas or stories from students, then my career would be complete. I'd be happy for the rest of my life. I saw myself sitting on a table in the front of a classroom, and there, sitting before me: curious learners.

I was, of course, mistaken in assuming that all my future learners would be curious and attentive.

Luckily, I didn't go the way of so many student teachers—preparation for the curious learner, confrontation with the alienated learner, then confusion, frustration, and predictably, departure from teaching. Intervention, in my case, came in the person of an education professor who knew that novelty and nonconformity could be the stuff of inspiration, a professor who provided a pathway to something beyond the assembly line method of education. The professor was Dr. Sterling Hennis. He knew that all human beings *are* inherently curious, and that the master teacher's task is to find the curiosity, the latent learning potential in a stu-

Inspiring Student Writers: Strategies and Examples for Teachers
pp. xiii–xiv

dent, and match tasks and activities to that potential so that a fire might be lit, as if by magic.

Hennis was my undergraduate advisor and then after I taught high school English for a year, I returned to grad school and became a teaching assistant under his tutelage. And there I met Tom Scheft, another of Hennis's teaching assistants. Tom and I shared an office and spent several productive and fun years under the guidance of our mentor. Hennis led us to the discovery that learning did not have to be stiff and sterile. He knew that a sure way to destroy a permanent reading or writing habit was to mandate rigid and uninspired requirements along with dull testing, testing, and more testing.

Tom and I both continued teaching and writing and loving our occupations. We've been very lucky that way. Sterling Hennis's inspiration was an early light that has led to the publication of *Inspiring Student Writers,* a book that announces how and why we should listen to (and march to) the voice from within the student.

While I've been involved in both teaching and writing for much of my adult life, I've learned that neither is a "higher" calling than the other. Teaching is harder, for me. Each profession offers opportunities, through stories, to consider and talk about relationships between people, right and wrong, good and evil, about matters of the heart, about passion.

Inspiring Student Writers helps students avoid The Great Modern Media Tragedy: the substitution of someone else's stories (Disney's, the textbook editor's, the TV commercial writer's) for their own stories.

Tom Scheft's ideas will ignite students. And that's what we all want—a lot of fire in the classroom.

PREFACE

Tom Scheft

This book evolved from a graduate class writing assignment several years ago. I've been teaching since 1971 and have been a teacher at North Carolina Central University (NCCU)—a historically Black school in Durham, North Carolina—since 1978. In 2002, towards the end of the fall semester—that time when grades are due and you're inundated with papers, papers, papers—I was thinking a thought common to many teachers: *Why the hell do I keep doing this job?* It's a question that comes up constantly in the lives of educators, and we deal with it in various ways— sometimes dropping out, sometimes burning out, typically soldiering on.

A friend and colleague, sensing my mood, sent me a book in which various educators selected a poem that most influenced them in their professional lives and then—briefly—reflected on it. Reading the book was, for me, an effective "shot in the arm," a "recharging of batteries," a positive reminder of why I chose (and keep choosing) the profession—a reaffirmation of why the hell I *want* to do the job.

As a graduate educational psychology teacher, I felt the book's concept—with a few alterations—would transfer well to my course, allowing my students to deal with psychological concerns in a personal, meaningful, realistic manner. It would tap in to what motivated them and, through development and revision, get them to reveal more about themselves,

Inspiring Student Writers: Strategies and Examples for Teachers
pp. xv–xviii
Copyright © 2009 by Information Age Publishing

especially how they worked with other students. So I created a writing assignment. My students—classroom teachers, special educators, counselors, mental health workers, and library/media coordinators—did the assignment ... and it was good. Indeed, their work was remarkable—often inspiring.

After a few semesters and some impressive work by my students, I thought, *Hmmm. I've got a book here. All I have to do is assemble some of the best pieces.* I paused. *You're a genius,* I said to myself. *Thank you,* I replied.

A lot of publishers liked the idea, but they wouldn't commit beyond that. However, when I talked with Dr. Patty Ruggiano Schmidt of Information Age Publishing, she liked the idea, but she wanted more than a book of student pieces. She wanted me to develop the book around my theoretical base as a teacher of writing. "Can you talk about *how* you work with students? Can you provide some analysis of their work?" she asked.

Okay. I could do that. And if I did, the book would be published. I'd get my students' work to a larger audience and offer some valuable information to my fellow educators. So even though this is not my original idea—a book of inspirational writing, it *is* that ... and more. You get motivational pieces that engage and excite and uplift—whoever you are, whatever you do. For the teachers out there, you get some effective writing strategies for students, some time-tested tools for building effective writers, and an explanation of how to structure a motivational, reflective assignment that can lead to some inspiring work. And if you act *now,* I'll throw in a set of steak knives!

This book's title notes strategies and examples. The strategy part comes in the first three chapters. In the first chapter, I describe my approach to writing with students by discussing the people and ideas that influenced me. In chapter 2, Dr. Sandy Vavra, a professor in the NCCU Department of English and a teacher of writing, discusses the positive research on students writing about their lives and experiences. In chapter 3, I explain my motivational writing assignment, which is followed by specific examples in chapters 4-16. An appendix includes three articles that discuss helping students understand and avoid stereotypes, assisting student writers in coping with rejection, and dealing with dialect differences in the classroom.

Let me explain why I've included those pieces. When students read and discuss characters and cultures, when students write and create characters, it is quite common for stereotypes to emerge. Students talk about and write about stereotypical characters doing stereotypical things because their minds are filled with stereotypical situations borne of the media (TV, movies, music, magazines, and so on), conversations with others, and family/community values. Forming stereotypes is part of our thinking process as humans. One can understand this by studying the theories and research of famed psychologist Jean Piaget. Stereotyping is a natural thing that we, as humans, do. Don't misunderstand. I'm not condoning stereotyping. However, understanding how and why we do it is important. Many teachers, when confronting stereotypical thinking in students, get flustered and unsure of what to do, or they get angry and overreact. I present "Confronting Stereotyping: Understanding Why We Do It, Considering What to Do About It" as a proactive, assertive response that deals with writing but goes beyond that into critical thinking.

I include "Helping Student Writers Understand and Deal with Rejection" for all our students who want to be "the next big thing." Being a successful writer means having to cope with rejection ... and lots of it. This is another proactive piece that underscores the importance of perseverance in coming to grips with the harshness of writing as a business. The chapter provides insight about and by two successful writers.

The last chapter, "Dealing with Dialect Differences: Honest Concerns and Practical Approaches," speaks to a classroom and societal issue that can have devastating consequences on students as writers and speakers. This chapter ties in with the aforementioned topics of stereotyping and rejection, providing a perspective on dialect prejudice and offering strategies for educating students (and anyone else who needs it—*which includes a whole lot of adults*). Dialect is a controversial topic in education and throughout society that many teachers, administrators, and parents typically avoid—often out of ignorance.

CHAPTER 1

WORKING WITH STUDENT WRITERS

Tom Scheft

I have always believed it is important for students to write and receive feedback on their work. Constructive, detailed feedback is crucial to improvement. I came to understand this early in life because of my mom—who would talk over my writing assignments with me, guide me through the composing, point out strengths and weaknesses, and get me to revise. I really appreciated her role, even though I didn't always enjoy the work. But she taught me to value the power and artistry of writing. Eventually she, with the assistance of some other fine teachers, helped me grow to love writing and understand that good writing is rewriting ... often again and again and again. As a teacher, she was firm and patient with me. Beyond that, she also subtly (and if you know my mom, some-times *not* so subtly) pushed me to do better, to be more creative, to excel.

Okay, Mom, I *got* it.

When I became a teacher, I adopted her role as writing coach for my students. And like so many other teachers, I have been on a continual mission to get my students to like, even love, writing, to get them to make their work appealing and powerful, to discover the aspects of their lives worth writing about—not just for themselves, but for an audience "out

Inspiring Student Writers: Strategies and Examples for Teachers
pp. 1–16
Copyright © 2009 by Information Age Publishing

1

there," in their families, their schools, their communities ... and beyond. I try to make my students see themselves as writers.

Thirty-five years after I taught her in seventh grade, one of my students read about me in the paper and contacted me through e-mail, told me she was a professional writer (Elizabeth McDavid Jones), and said I had inspired her way back when. (Hey, she was an *unbelievable* writer. My part was easy.) She added that she had dedicated her first book to me. (Yes, I am smiling as I write this.) I have worked with other spectacular student writers throughout my career, and those with talent I have encouraged to publish their work—typically through newsletters, newspapers, magazines, journals, handouts, and Internet postings.

So what exactly guides my approach with student writers? There are three key aspects:

1. The contemporary theory of Constructivism and the Writing Process (Nonteachers, you may not be familiar with those terms. If your eyelids are feeling heavy, hang in there; this will be pretty painless.);
2. The learning theory of Robert Gagné (I know. You never heard of him. Stay with me.); and
3. The New Journalism, especially the contributions of premier new journalist and best-selling novelist Tom Wolfe.

CONSTRUCTIVISM AND THE WRITING PROCESS

Contemporary educational psychology textbooks define Constructivism in a broad sense, as focusing on *active* learning through which a student builds understanding and makes sense of information. Constructivism echoes an old saying, "We learn by doing," and if we apply this to writing, it means—quite simply—students need to write. Pretty obvious, huh? Unfortunately, a lot of students *don't* write ... or don't write very much ... or have little to no guidance when writing.

Constructivism also speaks to *authentic* writing. This means that if we want students to be writers, we need to treat them like real writers; they need to behave like real writers. (Don't misunderstand. I'm not advocating giving students fifths of liquor and exhorting them to furnish Faulknerian prose.) For students to compose like actual, paid-for-a-living, professional writers, they need to follow the writing process:

1. The first step is *brainstorming*. This may include reading, researching, note taking, discussion, and just plain, good old thinking. Author James Thurber once quipped that he worked diligently try-

ing to convince his wife that—when he was (seemingly) gazing mindlessly out the window—he was *working*. (Now that's a story worth sticking to.)

In 1992, novelist Clyde Edgerton took a trip to Mesa Verde in Colorado, where he became fascinated with the cliff dwellings and excited by the dramatic story of the young Swedish anthropologist who wrote about them. While teaching and working on other projects, Edgerton researched the subject *for a year*—reading 40 books and taking 500 pages of notes. During that time an idea for a novel was taking shape in his mind, a book he would work on for 2 years—*Redeye: A Western*.

2. Then comes writing *the first draft*—which may be a swooping, get-it-all-out approach or a more measured, write-and-polish method ... or a combination of both.

3. Next is *feedback*, which could come from peers, adults, teachers, or all of the above.

4. After that is *revision*.

5. Then comes *additional feedback*.

Steps 4 and 5 could be repeated again and again, depending on the nature of the writing and the time frame. Revision is the time for correcting, deleting, and/or adding (new drafting). It's also a time for content to be polished ... and polished and polished and polished.

6. The next step is *publishing the finished piece*.

7. The next logical stage is *circulating the material* and/or *presentation by the author*.

I often have my university students read their work aloud. Many elementary schools perform this step very effectively with a culminating experience like an authors' tea—complete with readings, an audience of other classes and parents, refreshments, printed programs, and even an autograph session.

It is often at the conclusion of the process, after all parts have been completed, after all the teacher's pushing, prompting, prodding, insisting, threatening, bribing, cajoling, guiding ... after all the student work (the drafting, correcting, revising, polishing, muttering under his/her breath) ... that—*finally*—all the time and effort make sense. Some students look back on the journey and they "get it." They know what it takes for *them* to do quality work, and they will forever change the way they write. *Some* students.

Now many teachers will tell you, "I have my students write." But they don't follow the writing process, so students aren't behaving like *real* writers. Traditional classroom writing methods often truncate the process, leave out important steps, collapse it into a class period (or less)—rendering it no process at all. Here is what you might expect an elementary school teacher to say:

> Good morning, children. We've been studying the farm for two weeks now, and I've got a wonderful concluding exercise for you. Each of you will get a sheet of this special paper. See! I've cut it out in the shape of a baby chicken. Now, I want each of you to write about why you'd like to be a baby chicken. Make sure you write neatly, because you may only have one piece of paper. I'll collect these in fifteen minutes. Begin. Oh ... and be creative!

A middle grades teacher might approach a writing assignment this way:

> To prepare you for the end-of-grade writing test, I want all of you to write a 5-paragraph argumentative paper on how to improve the food in the cafeteria. Make sure your first sentence explicitly states your main point and includes three specific points. Make sure your second paragraph expands your first example in at least two sentences. Make sure your third paragraph expands your second example in at least two sentences. Make sure your fourth paragraph expands your third example in at least two sentences. Make sure your fifth paragraph or conclusion restates your first paragraph. You have the rest of the period to complete this. Begin.
>
> Oh! Before you start, a reminder: Two spelling errors is an automatic F. Each comma splice lowers your grade by one letter. A sentence fragment is an automatic D. A subject-verb agreement error ...

As with the above examples, the sterility and intimidation of many classroom writing programs and assignments can be deflating and disheartening to aspiring authors (never mind the "I hate to write" student), but there are various ways to get students writing about things that matter to them, while also experimenting with different styles, techniques, and tones. Journal writing, which I use in all my classes, is a popular, effective method for writing experimentation. Entries don't always have to be in essay form; students can create commercials, dramatic sketches, film treatments, stream of consciousness, poetry, scripts, and reviews.

In addition to involving students in the writing process, we need to remind them frequently that they are *real* writers, doing the same things professional writers do—including dealing with various kinds of frustration, such as others not liking or understanding their work, and having to revise multiple times in order for a piece to be good. Another aspect of writing authentically is learning to face and handle rejection. (In this book's appendix, I discuss a very successful writer, Clyde Edgerton, who *almost* gave in to rejection, who *almost* gave up writing fiction.)

There is, technically, no set limit to the cycles of revision and feedback. While he was teaching college and writing other novels and short stories, Edgerton spent 10 years working on what many consider a masterpiece, *The Floatplane Notebooks*. The book went through 50 drafts—some big and some small. As a writer, Clyde typically composes several versions of a final novel, along with preliminary notes and outlines, so that the paperwork for each novel takes up a full filing cabinet drawer. *Floatplane*, however, takes up three filing cabinet drawers and two trunks. As a college teacher, I have my students for a semester. I don't have a lot of time to work with them.

When my students write, I am their editor—to point out, to prod, to push, to criticize constructively, to encourage, to question. I am there to help them revise. Sounds simple enough, but having taught for over 30 years, I can safely say most students I've worked with *do not like to revise*. (Hey, I don't like to revise. Who does?) But it is a critical part of the process. Revision helps bad writing become better. It can turn good writing into excellent writing. It's never easy. It's rarely quick. But it is a necessary, indispensable part of the process.

A good editor does more than use red ink to point out spelling, punctuation, and usage concerns. And look: I don't agree with the anti-red ink brigade—that you're "bleeding" on the paper, that you're saying "stop" to the student. I like red ink. It shows up effectively on the page. Red means love; red means passion. I am a caring, concerned dude who wants to help you improve. So read my red comments. They'll help you.

A good editor engages with the piece—looking for answers to a number of questions:

- Does the paper communicate clearly, effectively?
- Does it *grab* the reader, bother, annoy, move the reader?
- Are the points clear?
- Are the examples powerful, convincing, vivid?
- Are more examples needed?
- Is the paper interesting and/or relevant and/or useful?
- Are the sources convincing and contemporary?
- Do the characters "come alive"?
- Is something missing?

- Are you telling your audience something they already know, "preaching to the choir"?
- Is the sentence structure effectively varied?
- Is the tone (mood) clearly conveyed?
- Are the word choices thoughtful, engaging, precise?

Okay, that's enough. You might think of others. As editor, I must ask those questions, point out strengths and weaknesses, offer suggestions and, when appropriate, provide answers. I must communicate—orally and/or on paper—the good, the bad, and the ugly. In addition to copy-editing, I provide separate, computer-generated comments—a document for the writer to read, refer to, and—if necessary—read again. After that, the writer needs the opportunity to revise—fixing mechanics and usage, incorporating the suggestions, deleting the ineffective and adding the effective. And then the revised work comes back to me (or others) for further scrutiny, which—as mentioned before—could be one step ... or two steps ... or three ... or ... .

Revision is particularly difficult with students who don't like to write, because ... *they don't like to write.* And they are the ones who really need to revise—often a number of times. As you go beyond simple correcting to having them elaborate on their ideas, you are often confronted by statements like: "Gee, what do you expect me to do—*write a book*?!" I usually smile and say, "No ... not a book. But how about a better paper?"

Stay firm. After all, you're asking them to do something they don't like to do. Make sure the students save each version of the paper (physical, powerful evidence of how the piece has evolved). Keep pushing for clarity and development. Eventually your persistence will pay off. Will you have transformed the student? Not likely. But some do change their writing habits. They see they can do quality work, and they now understand what it takes to produce material of that caliber.

My favorite story about revising a paper involved a very reluctant student who was writing about his adolescence and how he and his father were constantly at odds. The writer, a Black man looking back over three decades, reminisced proudly about his teenage social consciousness in the 1960s—contrasting it with his memory of a father who kowtowed to Whites. He still bore a disdain for his father's fawning ways with White folks.

The first version of the paper was fairly sketchy. I wanted clearer examples of what the father did that angered the son so much. That proved difficult for the writer. As I keep after him to develop his ideas, something strange happened. When he tried to flesh out certain events, he couldn't come up with details, and this caused him to wonder about the validity of his memories. Suddenly, he started remembering things about his father he'd forgotten. One particular memory emerged from when the author was 6 years old. He was with his parents in a store where his dad made weekly payments on the living room furniture:

> The store workers made Blacks wait until the Whites were served before taking our money. On one occasion, my dad saw a large Black lady in tears standing by the WHITE restroom. As I watched, I realized she had urinated on herself. He walked over to her and angrily said, "Why did you not go in before you did this on yourself?" Dad pulled the "WHITE" sign off the door and demanded, "Go in there and clean up." Dad stood at the door until the lady came out. Then he walked back over to mom and me. As a 6-year-old, I did not fully realize what was happening. I do remember my mother holding my hand so very tight, like a vise, in fear of what might happen to my dad. I do not remember seeing the signs on the bathroom doors after that day. I would like to think, as a result of my Dad's actions, the "COLORED" signs were removed in that store.

With this memory came a radical shift in the paper. What started out as a smug, disparaging recollection turned to critical self-reflection:

> While I used to be upset that my dad was not directly involved in the Civil Rights Movement, I understand now Dad was doing what he considered he had to do to keep his job, feed his family, and keep a roof over our heads ... So often I talked mean to my dad, as if belittling him would change his way of talking to Whites. I had no consideration of the way he felt.
>   The things I did as a teen to signify that I was a strong Black American only hurt me in the terms of being a servant to my race or to better my own growth as a Black man in American society. My father died before I could apologize to him. I try to make up for my actions by treating all people as I expect to be treated. I try to have love and compassion for all walks of life. As I work toward being a good counselor, I must have knowledge of the cultures, beliefs, and environmental conditions that cause people to act and react as they do.

As the paper changed dramatically through revision, it was clear that certain "facts" turned out to be distortions, while other forgotten elements—like the powerful scene in the furniture store—emerged. For the author, a tough, no-nonsense man who had been a former prison guard, this writing was a paradoxical process—difficult, yet enlightening; rewarding, yet troubling.

"I don't want to read this in class," he said. "I'm afraid what my classmates will think of me."

I assured him it would go well. "This paper says a lot about how people change, about the stages they go through," I said. "It speaks to all of us. It is very moving."

And that is the effect it had on his peers, even though they didn't hear the whole paper. The author broke down and was unable to read the last two sentences.

THE LEARNING THEORY OF ROBERT GAGNÉ

I'm going to simplify this a lot, but I don't think R.G. will be upset. If you want students to learn, says Gagné in *The Conditions of Learning and Theory of Instruction* (1985), you need to make things *interesting, relevant,* and *useful.* Certainly we can extend this advice to authors and their audience. If you can make your work interesting, relevant, and useful, you will attract, hold, and captivate the reader.

Okay. There you go. Can we move on?

Not quite. While those three adjectives are useful guides for composing any kind of work, they are very subjective terms, especially the word "interesting." One person's "interesting" is another person's "boring." Some people love to garden. I'll opt for the root canal instead.

Understanding that "interesting" is an elusive term, having your audience relate to your piece will certainly engage them. And if they can't initially relate, can they see how what you have to say is useful to them? If they can apply your message to their lives, that keeps them connected. Interesting, relevant, useful—if you can get your audience to connect with all three, you've forged a strong bond. And two out of three ain't bad either.

Gagné's theory provides a link to another contemporary term: culturally responsive pedagogy, which means—simply—that teaching can be effective when students see how it relates to their culture. Well sure. There you go. Now can we move on?

Not quite. Oftentimes teachers *think* they're being culturally responsive, but they're not. Consider the work of researchers Moll and Diaz. In the early 1980s, public school teachers in San Diego, particularly high school English teachers, were concerned with motivating bilingual Hispanic students to improve their writing. Moll and Diaz's early observations noted little evidence of writing at home except for a few practical purposes: making grocery lists, taking phone messages, and writing letters. Initially, Moll and Diaz proposed that teachers build on these uses, but the teachers argued this kind of writing was not particularly demanding and would not help students master the advanced writing skills of secondary and college-level education.

More interviews and observation by the researchers uncovered that the parents valued education, were supportive of the schools, and considered the development of writing skills essential for their children. In addition, the researchers learned that social issues *within the Hispanic culture*—unemployment, immigration, racism, and the need to learn English—were compelling for the students. This information was used to create writing modules that focused on those concerns. The modules were successful, because the students were hooked on the relevancy of the topics; they saw the writing as purposeful and were motivated to apply advanced writing techniques (e.g., developing questionnaires, surveying and recording opinions, writing analytically) to their pieces—skills they could use in other classes and in furthering their education.

I can hear you thinking: *What does this have to do with culture? Writing teachers have been forever telling students: "Find something you want to write about, something important to you."*

True. But in the past, when these topics emerged from the Hispanic students, the majority of their teachers, *who were outside of Hispanic culture*, found the topics too controversial and, thus, avoided them or discouraged them or even refused to deal with them. This reaction may remind many of reports in the late 1960s, when teachers saw certain African American students who "could not read" totally engrossed in *The Autobiography of Malcolm X*. There was a common response: "How can this student read this book, when he can't read the material I give him?"

The difference was interest, relevance, and usefulness.

TOM WOLFE AND THE NEW JOURNALISM

In the late 1970s I accepted a position in the English Department at North Carolina Central University, as part of the new Media-Journalism Program. The program's director, Dr. Andrew "Mac" Secrest, an award-winning editorial writer and civil rights activist, was a great boss to work for—wonderfully encouraging and supportive of new things I wanted to try. At this time I stumbled upon *The New Journalism* by Tom Wolfe, a collection of the genre's memorable pieces by writers like Wolfe, Joe Eszterhas, George Plimpton, Gay Talese, Jimmy Breslin, Truman Capote, Joan Didion, Hunter Thompson, and others. The articles instantly captivated me. I was also intrigued by Wolfe's explanation of how these contemporary non-fiction writers were, in many cases, eclipsing the impact of novelists. These "new" journalists were anything but the stereotypical notion of the non-fiction writer. As Wolfe (1973) noted, you'd be reading one of their non-fiction pieces and wondering: *"What the hell is going on?* With a little reworking the whole article could have read like a short story" (p. 11). Wolfe described his own transformation as a writer:

What interested me was not simply the discovery that it was possible to write accurate non-fiction with techniques usually associated with novels and short stories. It was that—plus. It was the discovery that it was possible in non-fiction, in journalism to use any literary device, from the traditional dialogisms of the essay to stream-of-consciousness, and to use many different kinds simultaneously, or within a relatively short space … to excite the reader both intellectually and *emotionally*. (p. 15)

Of the basic "tools" he discussed and illustrated, I saw four in particular that could help transform student writing:

1. *Scene-by-scene construction*—taking the reader through the experience, providing a sense of detail, depth, and immediacy. Such thorough re-creation helps readers feel a part of the situation, as though they are eavesdropping or eyewitnesses. For many student writers this is drudgery. "Do I have to take you through *everything* that happened?" Sometimes the answer is "yes." It is necessary to provide an authentic account; the reader will be grateful.

I remember working with a superb special education teacher who was writing about her job. "You need to tell the *whole* story," I kept saying to her. "You need to *show* the readers your job. They don't have a clue. Write what happens—*exactly* what happens during the day. It's not hard. It's just going to take some time."

And she did. And when a good special education teacher takes you scene-by-scene through the job—through the distinct, different student personalities; the individual learning challenges; the regulations and restrictions; the routines; the behavioral "train wrecks"; and the triumphs (usually tiny, sometimes extraordinary), you realize you couldn't do that job for one day … let alone one hour.

2. The use of *brief physical description*—enough to help the reader conjure up a vision of the characters, rendering them as real images, rather than faceless ideas. When we read about people, we need to see them through our mind's eye. Given the cognitive demands of reading, helping shape a character's image is a writer's *responsibility*.

When we watch a movie, we interact with the collaborative product of legions of talented professionals—actors, writers, directors, cinematographers, producers, consultants, set designers, carpenters, electricians, dialogue coaches, musicians, sound effects folks, stylists, wardrobe people, stunt crews, painters, special effects designers, editors … and more. Watching that finished work, compared to reading, is *easy*. With print, all we've got is a squiggly, symbolic code on a page. From that, if we're really good, we become the actors, director, and all those other aforementioned roles. That's not easy.

Don't misunderstand. I love reading. But it's really hard. I don't have any problem watching a film for two hours. But I rarely read for two straight hours. After one hour, I'm pretty drained.

The reader needs help, although Wolfe (1973) notes "writers have a hard time even creating a picture of a human. Detailed descriptions tend to defeat their own purpose, because they break up the face rather than create an image" (p. 48). Fine. But the writer still needs to throw the reader a visual bone ... or two ... or three. Color. Texture. Shape. Detail. *Something*. Otherwise, how are we supposed to develop an image of Aunt Tillie ... or Bobby ... or Shanika ... or Juan ... or Veruska ... without— perhaps—indulging in the most obvious stereotypes? Besides, as a writer, you don't need to do a lot:

> Jimmy was my best friend when we were 17. He wore a constant smirk on his freckled face, framed by a sweep of thick brown hair. He was a wise guy—not the organized crime type, the smart-ass type, Eddie Haskell come to life. He was a superb athlete, but not with a big, muscled body; his was lean and flexible. He had a scar on his left cheek—a jagged, red, claw-like thing, a remnant from a car accident—that might have looked awful on anybody else, but it actually worked for him. It made him vulnerable ... dangerous ... not perfect ... all of the above. Girls dug that scar. Lots of girls.

*   *   *

> Darryl walked slumped over, eyes cast downward. You didn't see them except—maybe—fleetingly. His skin was smooth like a 6-year-old's, even though he was sixteen. He didn't appear to have ever shaved. He went through life slumped over, eyes down. And his hair ... You could imagine Einstein saying, "Look, it's none of my business ... but you need to do something with that."

As a writer of characters (real or fictional), you need to provide some description. It doesn't take a lot. Your audience will be grateful.

3. *Status-life detail*. This is Wolfe's term and a wonderful complement to physical detail. It is the notion that when possible, description should help convey a sense of socioeconomic status (financial and educational level), even a sense of the *zeitgeist* (spirit of the times). You do more than say someone is wearing a blue, button-down shirt. Does it come from J.C. Penney or Nordstrom's? Is it newly purchased, professionally laundered, obtained from a thrift store, shoplifted?

Wolfe (1973) describes the device as

> the recording of everyday gestures, habits, manners, customs, styles of furniture, clothing, decoration, styles of traveling, eating, keeping house, modes of behaving toward children, servants, superiors, inferiors, peers, plus the

various looks, glances, poses, styles of walking and symbolic details that might exist within a scene ... Symbolic, generally of people's *status life*, using that term in the broad sense of the entire pattern of behavior and possessions through which people express their position in the world or what they think it is or what they hope it to be. (p. 32)

Wolfe loves to pile on lines and lines and lines (example after example after example) of status life detail—connecting with readers, jogging their memories, sparking images in their minds. You don't need to be as exhaustive as Wolfe. For example, if I were using status-life detail to portray me at the ripe old age of 6, I'd write:

First grade was hard, and so I was in no rush to walk to Pierce School. I'd slowly amble down Exeter Street, cross over Commonwealth Avenue. I'd watch the Italian gardeners—mowing, raking, clipping the expansive lawns. They didn't have to go to school. So lucky. They got to cut grass, work with their shirts off. They bought chocolate or strawberry milk from the milkman, then drank it ... *right out of the bottle*. So lucky. I'd swing my Roy Rogers lunch box, listening to the apple bang against the tuna sandwich in wax paper and thermos of milk (*plain* milk) the maid packed, as I shuffled along in my black, high-top Keds.

If I described myself at age 12, I'd talk about tight black "chinos" (khaki pants), Weejun loafers, and heavy doses of Brylcream in my hair. I'd reference playing sports and discovering girls for the first time. Growing up in an affluent family, I'd mention going to dance class on Friday nights.

When discussing age 16, I'd mention Levi bell-bottom jeans (honest), brown suede Beatle boots from Thom McAn (a shoe store), hot-combing my wavy hair to make it straight (so it would look more like the rock stars I admired), and growing sideburns below my ears. I'd talk about getting into rock music, being in a band, using Slingerland drums that my parents bought me, and listening to the Beatles, Stones, Kinks, Love, and Paul Revere and the Raiders. I'd talk about going to prep school.

DIALOGUE

Says Wolfe (1973), dialogue "involves the reader more completely than any other single device. It also establishes and defines character more quickly and effectively than any other single device" (p. 31).

There is an art to creating good dialogue, or in the case of nonfiction, getting people to speak effectively (without putting words in their mouth). This can be a problem nowadays, as so much colloquial conversation is not specific. You know what I mean? People start talking about something … You know where I'm comin' from? And it's like, you know, they … um … start and everything and they're sorta kinda explaining … You know what I'm sayin'? And … whatever.

I trust that was helpful.

As humans, we understand each other on a *general* level:

"So I'm talking with my 16-year-old son."

"These kids today."

"Tell me about it."

"I hear you."

"Like the world revolves around him."

"That's what I'm talking about."

"Like I was put on this earth to be his personal servant."

"Ummm … ummm … um."

We "communicate" in this fill-in-the-blanks, clichéd, contemporary shorthand. It's ubiquitous. And often when we *try* to write, the transition from vapid chitchat, from undeveloped thoughts to something clear, something salient is *hard*.

SHOWING … NOT JUST TELLING

Good communication requires more than stitching together generalities.

Someone's job is boring? What—exactly—does that mean? Your friend is "so funny." Really? Well, help me out here. *Convince* me. You are a creative, caring, compassionate, witty, brilliant, wonderful human being. Ohkay … Look; it's not that I don't believe you, but … what makes you so creative, caring, compassionate, witty, brilliant, and wonderful? You need to show me.

My mother loves to tell the story of a postcard my brother John, age 8, sent from summer camp:

Dear Mom and Dad,

The most interesting thing happened at camp today.

Love,
John

The best writers show us—typically using the techniques previously mentioned. It's not enough to say your child is precocious. Ninety-six-point-three percent of parents think that about their children:

> I drive my 6-year-old son to school. I try to be a responsible father, engaging him in conversation, getting him talking. And I am amazed with some of the ideas and expressions that come out of his mouth. I mean ... he is just so precocious ... like he's 6 going on 26.

Can we relate? Sure. But what happens when we apply a little description, status life detail, inner thoughts, and dialogue. True story:

> I drive my 6-year-old son to school everyday. And I'm Ward Cleaver. I'm the guy on "Father Knows Best." I'm Dr. Cliff Huxtable. I engage him, get him talking, because I'm going for Parent-of-the-Millennium. It's my quest.
>
> But Daniel—Mr. Backwards Hat, Mr. Why Can't We Listen to Music? (and not your classic rock crap, Dad), Mr. I Don't Feel Like Talking, Mr. I'd Rather Play with My Action Figures, Mr. Dad, Why Are You Ruining My Life? ... freakin' kid can't appreciate my mentoring.
>
> "Daniel," I say, "let's talk."
>
> "Aw, Dad, do we have to?"
>
> "Yes," I say firmly, thinking: WHY DO WE KEEP PLAYING THIS GAME? "Dan, why do we keep playing this game?"
>
> No answer. He turns his Nike-covered body away from me.
>
> His straight blond/brown hair peeks out from his hat. COME UP WITH SOMETHING GOOD, I think, realizing I'm unprepared. "Okay ... so let's talk about animals."
>
> "What about them?"
>
> IGNORE THE ATTITUDE. IGNORE THE ATTITUDE. "Okay ... so if you could be any animal, what would you choose?"
>
> "What do you mean 'any animal'?"
>
> "Any animal ... a lion ... a snake ..."
>
> "Dad, a snake isn't an animal. It's a reptile." He turns to me. "What? You didn't *know* that?"
>
> "Yes, I *knew* that. I was talking generally. So ... what would you choose?"
>
> He thinks for a moment. "A dog."
>
> "A dog? You don't like dogs."
>
> "Yeah, but I wouldn't mind being one. You can run really fast. You can bark at people. You have sharp teeth."
>
> He sinks back into the car seat, then sort of bounds up, twisting his body to fully face me. "Hey, Dad, what did the elephant say to the naked man?"
>
> "Uh, I don't know."
>
> "How do you *breathe* through that thing?"

You'll notice I didn't use the words "precocious" or "funny." You don't need to tell when you show.

EDUCATIONAL WRITING

I don't know many folks who keep educational journals on their bedside tables. I can't remember hearing anyone say, "You have *got* to read this article this professor wrote! It's incredible." Or … "Free tickets to the Super Bowl? Gee, normally I'd like to go, but my new *Journal of Psychological Abstracts* just came in the mail." There is a lot of educational writing out there. And I'm not saying it's all bad, but ….

When I moved to the School of Education, I wanted to take a different approach to "educational writing"—what it had to sound like, what it had to focus on. I knew firsthand the powerful, important, relevant things that go on in the lives of educators and students. I knew they had stories to tell—experiences that would educate, motivate, and even inspire. I knew many did jobs that the vast majority of us (me included) couldn't do. And I knew I could help them tell their stories.

"BUT I'M NOT A WRITER"

It's paradoxically amusing and maddening how we form concepts about life. As the famed cognitive theorist Jean Piaget reasoned, we are born with the innate ability to find meaning in life through sorting and arranging information. This ongoing process begins early and stays with us until death. Our motivation? *We want to make sense of the world.*

Ironically, while the process does help us cope and succeed, it also explains our tendency to stereotype. The more information we have, the more we remove the tendency to generalize. But judgments made with little information or false information, well … that's how stereotypes are born. We grow up seeing a certain image (or *not* seeing a certain image), and after a while, we may tend to believe it is "true," even if it's a distorted image. Why? *Because we want to make sense of the world.*

Many of us grow up with the image, the notion, the stereotype of "a good writer"—some old, White guy smoking a pipe and wearing a tweed jacket with elbow patches who uses big words and writes things we don't understand. And because we *don't* understand his writing, well … then it must be good, right?

There are writers like that. But it stands to reason that a good writer, a great writer would also be one who *connects* with others … with us. That definition fits a lot of people, including many of my students. But they don't consider themselves writers. I'll often hear a student say: "I can't write." Translation: I don't use big words. Or … I don't write things that people don't understand. Or … I make mistakes sometimes. Or … what's so special/important/worth listening to about me? Or … my writing isn't complicated. (It just sounds "normal.") Or ... my papers don't sound like William Styron ... or Shakespeare ... or Toni Morrison. Or ... I don't fit my preconception of a writer. (I'm not old, White, male ...)

But *through the writing process*, a good many of my students—albeit reluctantly—come to say to themselves: *I can write.*

And they also tell themselves: *I am a writer ... a really good writer.*

The road to that realization isn't all that hard; it's not tricky. As their guide, I show them—or reacquaint them with—a few techniques. They put in some time and effort, working their way through the process. And eventually, as they bask in the approval of their audience, as they engage in the questions and discussion their writing has stimulated, as they see the payoff to their hard work, they experience a significant insight: Their writing is a tremendous catalyst for awareness, for outrage, for concern, for tears, for laughter, for change. Their writing can touch hearts and minds. Their writing can spark epiphanies. It can motivate, jump start, wake up, kick butt. Their writing can make a difference.

Sometimes writing is hard. Sometimes it's fulfilling. Sometimes it's a drag. It is a talent many students have hidden, dormant. We need to help them discover it. We need to help them master it. They need to write. They need to engage in the writing process. They need our feedback— editing, suggestions, criticism, praise, guidance, and encouragement.

The results can be magnificent.

CHAPTER SUMMARY

My approach with student writers incorporates Constructivism, the Writing Process, Robert Gagné's basic learning theory, and the Tom Wolfe-articulated strategies of the New Journalists.

Teachers need to have their students *behave like real writers*.

Teachers need to assign students writing and *review it like a real, concerned editor*. As editors, our role—among many things—is to correct, to question, to suggest, to support, and to inspire.

All students have stories to tell. Push them to see themselves as writers.

REFERENCES

Gagné, R. M. (1985). *The conditions of learning and theory of instruction* (4th ed.). New York: Holt, Rinehart & Winston.

Moll, L. C., & Diaz, S. (1987). Change as the goal of educational research. *Anthropology and Education Quarterly, 18*, 300-311.

Wolfe, T. (1973). *The new journalism.* New York: Harper & Row.

CHAPTER 2

AUTOBIOGRAPHY IN TEACHER PREPARATION

The Internally Persuasive Discourse That Speaks With Authority

Sandra A. Vavra

You can't teach what you don't know.

What you don't know can hurt you.

Know thyself.

While some may dismiss the statements above as mere platitudes, who would disagree with their common sense? Imagine hiring a tennis coach who had never played competitive tennis or signing on with a piano teacher of questionable talent who had never performed before an audience. You simply wouldn't—because no amount of mere studying about these pursuits can substitute for having experienced them as a practitioner *before* attempting to teach someone else to do so. Similarly, who can argue that ignorance makes you safer than knowledge, whether that

Inspiring Student Writers: Strategies and Examples for Teachers
pp. 17–29
Copyright © 2009 by Information Age Publishing

knowledge be of others' agendas and motivations, the inherent dangers in a situation, the potential consequences of our actions, or the possible harm we could unwittingly inflict upon self and others? Finally, why would the greatest minds, from Socrates to Shakespeare, posit that "the unexamined life is not worth living" and "to thine own self be true" as *common*, actionable wisdom throughout the centuries?

Surely, rather than platitudes, these statements are the stuff of solid folk wisdom, of *common* sense. Moreover, we should not dismiss or devalue them because they are in the *common* realm. Their *common*-ness shares much with the synonyms "united" and "familiar," and little with the pejorative synonyms "trite" and "hackneyed." There is something else these proverbial statements have in *common*: They serve as *common* themes which justify the use of autobiography as a highly effective (for some, even the preferred) method for learning: 1) which helps teachers reflect upon their teaching selves, attitudes, and biases; and 2) which immerses teachers in expressive writing in sufficient depth "to help teachers critically examine practices they might likely repeat" (Braun & Crumpler, 2004, p. 61)—in other words, to help them overcome the tendency to teach as they may have been mistaught (e.g., round robin reading of textbooks) rather than teach to students' needs.

Autobiography as inquiry has become an important educational practice in the past 2 decades (Conle, 1996; Mairs, 1994; Pinar, 1994; Raymond, Butt, & Townsend, 1992; Swindells, 1995; Witherell & Noddings, 1991)—fitting the postmodern notion of writing as bringing ideas into being that were not there before the act of writing. What makes this writing so compelling is that it conceives of *voice* as "a project involving appropriation, social struggle, and becoming" (Lensmire & Satanofsky, 1998, p. 284). In other words, it involves ongoing work to use the language we have acquired from society to discover our own voice, and to grow, sometimes at the risk of displeasing the society whose language we have appropriated as we challenge it.

A related line of research supports a variety of expressive writing genres which help shape both writing skills and attitudes toward teaching among pre-service candidates and graduate students in education. They include examining personal beliefs in light of education theories via theory logs (Brookfield, 1995; Pajares, 1992); personal histories of beliefs about learning and teaching (Holt-Reynolds, 1992; Mahurt, 1998); personal journals (Progoff, 1975); critical incident citing (Brookfield, 1987, 1995); personal philosophies (Hiemstra, 1988, 2001); discipline-specific autobiographies (Danielson, 1989; Rosenthal, 1991); and cultural autobiographies as a critical step in developing culturally sensitive pedagogy (Florio-Ruane, 1994, 1995; Schmidt, 1999). Indeed, the scholarship is wide-ranging and almost consistently enthusiastic about the ameliorative effect of using personal writing to foster deep professional reflection. (See Faith Shields' [2002] "Who Do We Think We Are? The Ethics and Politics of Autobiographical Curriculum" for counterarguments.) But is there a solid theoretical foundation on which to build this house?

A THEORETICAL FRAMEWORK FOR LEARNING THROUGH WRITING

Deriving from a number of giants in socio-cognitive psychology and composition, principally Britton, Bruner, Vygotsky, and Emig, the theory of learning through writing is supported by Britton's claim (1972) that events can be known, understood, and learned by giving them shape in language, and is strongly seconded by Emig's argument that writing taps all three possible modes of representing knowledge (enactive, ikonic, symbolic): "What is striking about writing is that, by its very nature, all three ways of dealing with actuality are simultaneously or almost simultaneously deployed" (1977, p. 124). According to Yinger (1985), subsequent research suggests that "processing information through multiple codes results in richer memories and representations than using either code alone (p. 22), enhancing learning by increasing "depth of processing" (Craik & Lockhart, 1972). Vygotsky (1934/1962) provides the intriguing notion that writing requires "deliberate semantics—deliberate structures of the web of meaning" (p. 100), which suggests that writing re-presents experience and even transforms it, and Bruner (1962) supplies the linchpin when he states that learning is not a direct dealing with the world, but rather a constructed reality which emerges from a personal interpretation of meaning in experience. All together, they provide a solid theoretical base from which researchers and educators have launched experiments in personal (expressive) writing and its effect on teaching practices and the development of writing skills.

YOU CAN'T TEACH WHAT YOU DON'T KNOW

It seems counterintuitive at first, but closer examination suggests that raw experience is not the best way to learn, particularly for teachers. In "Our Lives as Writers," Norman and Spencer (2005) explain the phenomenon as follows:

> Thus, the twelve or more years of educational experience that pre-service teachers bring into their professional preparation programs have formed their beliefs and values about teaching and learning. Evidence suggests that even if these belief systems are implicit, they serve to filter new information

as candidates attempt to make sense of curricula that may or may not mirror their personal experiences. If beliefs remain unexamined, new learning afforded by preparation courses may not influence their views or be applied to teaching contexts. (p. 26)

The work of other researchers supports their conclusion that writing about one's experiences invites learning to a significantly greater degree than experience and knowledge unexamined by symbolic representation (Britzman, 1986; Clark & Peterson, 1986; Hollingsworth, 1989; Kagan, 1992; Knowles & Holt-Reynolds, 1991; Pajares, 1992). Moreover, the pace of writing is well matched to the pace of learning. Unlike direct experience or hearing about knowledge (as in lectures),

> written speech is bound up with the inhibition of immediate synpractical connections. It assumes a much slower, repeated mediating process of analysis and synthesis, which makes it possible not only to develop the required thought, but even to revert to its earlier stages, thus transforming the sequential chain on connections in a simultaneous, self-reviewing structure. Written speech thus represents a new and powerful instrument of thought. (Luria & Yudovich, 1971, p. 118)

The result of this self-paced learning through writing is a re-presentation of knowledge—a transformation of experiences remembered which captures the thought and feeling of the original experiences, but also makes connections among seemingly unconnected bits of knowledge and suggests relationships between old information and knowledge being newly acquired.

As mentioned earlier, the form of writing used to best effect in developing knowledge about teaching and learning in pre-service teachers is narrative writing, particularly autobiography. These autobiographies are analogous to the writing of historians, who link historical events through both primary causal relationships of real-world events and through semantic relationships, which uncover the reasons behind the events and thus attach a logic to it. These stories of history, as with all stories, fulfill the goal of *understanding*, which is critical to the humanities and social sciences; in short, they "create the social contexts without which we could not live" (Alheit, 2005, p. 202). Bruner outlines the process as follows:

> Having translated or encoded a set of events into a rule-bound symbolic system, a human being is then able to transform that representation into an altered version that may but does not necessarily correspond to some possible set of events. It is this form of effective productivity that makes symbolic representation such a powerful tool for thinking or problem solving: the range it permits for experimental alteration of the environment without

having, so to speak, to raise a finger by way of trial and error. (Bruner, Oliver, & Greenfield, 1966, p. 37)

Thus far, we have discussed that writing about one's experience invites deep understanding of that experience with a minimum of bias, and that the form of writing which seems to elicit the most profound understanding of both self and circumstance is personal (autobiographical), narrative writing. Yet, despite the strong arguments and research in favor of using autobiography as a method of developing pre-service teachers' and also experienced educators' philosophies of teaching and pedagogical skills, writing about the self (e.g., one's K-12 and beyond schooling experience; one's beliefs about the purpose of education; one's ideas about culturally responsive education) still remains on the periphery of required experiences in teacher education programs. Since education is considered a "social science," an inherent scientific bias in the discipline may be responsible for favoring *transactional* writing (expository and persuasive), which *explains* phenomena, over *expressive* writing (the purview of the humanities), which seeks to *understand* phenomena. However, historians (whose discipline within universities has aligned itself with both the social sciences and the humanities) feel no such hard science vs. humanities split. Historians trust the "internal logic of narrative constructions, the inherent rationality of narrative structure" (Alheit, 2005, p. 203) because the logic of understanding (which is the goal of the humanities) trumps the mere explanation of cause (which is the goal of the hard sciences). Educators might well acquaint themselves with this debate and adopt the historians' view so that expressive writing can assume parity with the currently favored modes of transactional writing and become a more common activity in the curricula of teacher candidates and even veteran educators.

Another contributor to the marginalization of writing (expressive or otherwise) in teacher education programs is the foregrounding of reading over writing in state competencies. Even though state licensure standards for pre-service teachers indicate an awareness that writing is key to learning, the standards focus on instructing candidates to be effective teachers of reading rather than writing (Norman & Spencer, 2005). Since the curriculum cannot cover everything in depth and because schools of education pay most attention to what their accrediting bodies consider important, using precious curriculum time to allow candidates to reflect consistently and often in writing upon their attitudes toward teaching and how their total educational experience has contributed to these attitudes is regarded as a luxury they cannot afford. And, while room seems to have been made for adding at least one course in theory and pedagogy about reading at many universities, equivalent course additions in writing theory and pedagogy are not in as much evidence.

Thus, the essential ingredient of "knowing" writing—by means of the consistent practice of it—is often limited in teacher education programs to first-year composition courses and to a few research papers in various content courses throughout the program of study. Even English education majors are limited in the kinds of writing they are asked to produce, the narrow genre of literary analysis being their most-required product. Added to this, they generally receive minimal instruction in composition theory and pedagogy beyond what can be covered in a few weeks of a methods course. As a result, preservice teachers are dealt a triple blow:

- they are asked to practice writing (any kind of writing) minimally as compared to other skills;
- when they do write, the products they are asked to create are limited to a few genres and often to one audience (a teacher, subject-expert); and
- expressive writing like autobiographies, which help candidates to reflect deeply on their beliefs and which open candidates up to accepting new methods of teaching they may not have personally experienced, is largely absent from their requirements.

Is it any wonder that student teachers, as well as experienced teachers, often report they are reluctant to teach writing, and that their writing assignments are often limited to class starters of journal writing (designed mostly to keep students busy while attendance is taken) and essays of the kind they were expected to reproduce within their disciplines at the university? We must surely understand their reluctance. Just like the inexperienced tennis coach and the unseasoned piano teacher, *how can they teach* a skill or ever feel comfortable about teaching *something they do not know deeply themselves?*

WHAT YOU DON'T KNOW CAN HURT YOU (AND OTHERS)

The mismatch between the cultural backgrounds of public school teachers and their students is well documented. Snyder, Hoffman, and Geddes (1997) report that 90.7% of U.S. teachers self-describe as middle class and White. A number of educators have argued that providing opportunities for teachers to acquire self-knowledge, particularly through writing, during their program of study is essential to addressing this mismatch (Banks, 1994; Britzman, 1986; Schmidt, 1996, 1998, 1999; Willis & Hunter, in press). And, indeed, the mismatch can be successfully overcome. Gloria Ladson-Billings (1994, 1995) has written compelling accounts of White, middle-class teachers who have worked within the communities of their African American students to build relationships that resulted in increased achievement.

But the literature also includes an ongoing record of the achievement gap between White and minority students as well as a number of cautionary tales. Cooper and Holzman (1989), for example, describe the mindset of students whose home language is summarily dismissed and devalued by teachers in the name of teaching "standard" English: "[They] see standard English acquisition and school itself as the negation of the home (and of the street), its values the negation of their values, its skills hopelessly beside the point in a different—more pressing—context" (p. 165). Villanueva adds an ironic note, arguing that "[w]hen we demand a certain language, a certain dialect, and a certain rhetorical manner, we seem to be working counter to the cultural multiplicity we seek" (p. 183). Indeed, the curriculum in education programs seems to be creating considerable cognitive dissonance when they offer courses like "Diversity, Schooling, and Change"—which sensitize candidates to culturally relevant pedagogy, then fail to require consistent reinforcement of that pedagogy by ensuring those candidates experience diverse ways of communicating (e.g., writing in a variety of genres for multiple audiences and purposes) and alternative ways of teaching foundational skills (e.g., teaching writing in the context of dialects rather than a monolithic standard) during their course of study. We might even consider the notion that we are developing hypocrisy in our teachers if we do not acknowledge the "mismatches" between what we tell them is important (e.g., culturally relevant pedagogy) and what they actually practice while they are learning (e.g., limited experience with varieties of writing; limited, perhaps no opportunities to challenge the "superiority" of standard English and how it is taught). What we let slip through the cracks as we prepare teachers *can hurt them*, setting them up as irrelevant and hypocritical even before they step into the classroom. Donald McCrary (2005) illustrates how teachers (and the society which demands that teachers cover only the "standard" dialect in their classes) might be perceived as hypocritical and irrelevant by students whose home language is not considered "standard":

Hold up. I know what you gonna say. Talkin' that black English is okay at home and with your friends, but don't be speakin' that foolishness in school or at the j-o-b. And don't be tellin' no students they can speak that mess either. You want people (read: white) to think they ignorant? Right. Right. I hear you. I hear you. But let's be real. America loves itself some black English. Half the announcers on ESPN speak it, and I'm talkin' about the white dudes, too. Americans know more black English than they like to admit. Black English is intelligible and intelligent, and just because somebody tells you different, don't necessarily make it so. And that's what I want the academy to understand. My students don't speak no broken English. They speak a legitimate dialect that conveys legitimate meanings. (p. 74)

The fact that McCrary uses a hybrid discourse, which demonstrates complex linguistic abilities, makes the point even stronger. The "standard" dialect cannot claim that it, alone, is the legitimate and favored *lingua franca* in the United States. Candidates who are not exposed to possibilities like hybrid discourse or whose home language may have been dismissed and de-valued as much as the students described in the literature are not equipped to overcome their irrelevance or fight the hypocrisy inherent in teaching writing as if they lived in a homogeneous society. Opening them up, through the reflection that results from autobiographical writing and curricular changes which invite them to practice a greater range of discourse modes, may result in their allowing their own students to apply all their linguistic knowledge (from home and academy) to meaningful course content and learning (Gilyard and Richardson, 2001). And, it may help them to understand that all students, but especially those at-risk, have been given the impossible task of developing their academic voice (i.e., writing convincingly like an expert in the privileged discourse of the academy) when they are assigned discipline-specific writing tasks (like literary analysis). If such assignments are the sole way students can demonstrate their learning and thinking and writing skills, they are doomed forever to be academy outsiders, denied the right to develop authentic voices. In the meantime, if teachers are not given opportunities to confront their beliefs through methods like autobiographical writing, *what they don't know can hurt them and their students.*

KNOW THYSELF

Robert Fulghum (1995) describes a concept called *liminality*, which serves as a metaphor for the kind of learning claimed for autobiographical reflection:

Liminality is the word for the threshold moment, from the Latin root *limin*, meaning the centerline of the doorway. Liminality is the moment of crossing over. It describes the transitional phase of personal change, wherein one is neither in an old state of being or a new, and not quite aware of the implications of the event. All the stages of life include liminality. Life is nothing but moments of crossing over. Stitching these moments together into the comforting quilt of wisdom is the task of one's later years. Only with the passage of time, the accumulation of information about the similar experiences of others, and the opportunity to fit a given moment into the overall scheme of one's life does a threshold experience become understood. Then we know that the rite of passage is contained in a single move in a single moment. Upon reconsideration, we invest the past with meaning. (p. 30)

Stitching liminal moments together as a means of understanding their influence on who we are and what we believe is the task of autobiography. As a consciously applied tool for teacher reflection, it holds promise for shortening the time needed to attain "wisdom" from "one's later years" to one's formative years as a professional. We have argued earlier in this piece that to be unreflective has consequences. Schon (1987) concludes that the unreflective teacher is merely a skilled technician rather than a professional who can recognize what works and doesn't work in a class-room and then make the appropriate arrangements. On the other hand, Colton and Sparks-Langer (1993) argue that reflective teachers develop *self-efficacy*, the belief that they contribute positively to their students' lives, schools, and communities.

Claiming even greater potential for autobiographical writing, Alheit (2005) posits that those who write autobiography as a means of organizing their experience "also generate personal coherence, identity, a meaning to their life history, and a communicable, socially viable life world per-spective for guiding their actions" (p. 209). Moreover, he argues that this individual identity work is the essence of education and learning, and that, collectively, they can transform institutional frameworks. In other words, when we begin to become aware of the unquestioned certainties of our social existence, then social institutions begin to change. He goes so far as to label the learning generated by autobiographical writing as a "socially explosive force" (p. 210).

This force can help balance the current technical/rational approach inherent in most teacher education course work, "designed to develop a set number of teacher competencies and methodological skills," by allow-ing "moral deliberation about practices of teaching" (Rousmaniere, 2000. p. 91). It can keep candidates from "simply adopting others' ideas for classroom practice, or attempting to teach in ways that represent the learning theory they have encountered in teacher education courses, [by preparing them] to form their own beliefs that are grounded in their lived experiences" (Alvine, p. 10). It can allow "an examination of action apart from the pressures of performance [and make it] possible to examine the adequacy and effectiveness of one's efforts" (Yinger, p. 26). It "can help teachers and their students and families develop an understanding of and appreciation for differences in their classrooms and local community" (Schmidt, 1999, p. 339). It can change teachers who "prevent students from fully participating in academic discourse by erecting walls of linguis-tic tolerance" (McCrary, p. 75). It is a powerful force, indeed.

THE CHORUS THAT IS THE TEACHER'S OWN VOICE

As we conclude, it is instructive to recall Bakhtin's (1981) distinction between *authoritative discourses* and *internally persuasive discourses*:

> Authoritative discourse—the language of the disciplines and of academic writing, of society's official business, of the patriarchy—"demands that we acknowledge it, that we make it our own; it binds us, quite independent of any power it might have to persuade us internally ... its authority was already acknowledged in the past." Internally persuasive discourse is that used by individuals and small groups to speak about their own lives and experience; such discourse "is denied all privilege, backed up by no authority at all, and is frequently not even acknowledged in society" (p. 342). However, it "is of decisive significance in the evolution of individual consciousness." (as quoted in Elbaz-Luwisch, 2002, p. 406)

The use of autobiographical writing in teacher preparation courses is a powerful means of helping candidates develop their own internally persuasive voice—to know the experiences which have shaped their attitudes about learning, teaching, and knowing what students need deeply enough to change their attitudes, if necessary. If the lessons convey significant depth, the knowledge gained becomes what philosopher Eugene Gendlin (1978) calls a *felt sense*,

> the soft underbelly of thought ... a kind of bodily awareness that ... can be used as a tool ... a bodily awareness that encompasses everything you feel and know about a given subject at a given time.... It is felt in the body, yet it has meanings. It is body and mind before they split apart. (pp. 36, 165)

This deeply felt sense which guides beliefs and actions is the essence of professional growth as a teacher. Having claimed their identity anew through writing, teachers are then better prepared to appropriate the voice that results in authoritative discourse, which can challenge the "unquestioned certainties" of educational practice. The principled practice of teaching requires individuals who know themselves so well that they understand what they don't know well enough to teach responsibly, non-hypocritically, and with multicultural finesse. In short, autobiography can help ensure that teachers, like physicians, truly act on the credo "Do no harm."

REFERENCES

Alheit, P. (2005). Stories and structures: An essay on historical times, narratives, and their hidden impact on adult learning. *Studies in the Education of Adults, 37*(2), 201-212.

Alvine, L. (2001, February-March). Shaping the teaching self through autobiographical narrative. *The High School Journal, 84,* 5-12.

Bakhtin, M. (1981). *The dialogical imagination* (M. Holquist, Ed.). Austin: University of Texas Press.

Banks, J. (1994). *An introduction to multicultural education.* Boston Allyn & Bacon.

Braun, J. A., & Crumpler, T. P. (2004). The social memoir: An analysis of developing reflective ability in a pre-service methods course. *Teaching and Teacher Education, 20,* 59-75.

Brookfield, S. D. (1987). *Developing critical thinkers: Challenging adults to explore alternatives ways of thinking and acting.* San Francisco: Jossey-Bass.

Brookfield, S. D. (1995). *Becoming a critically reflective teacher.* San Francisco: Jossey-Bass.

Britton, J. (1972). *The humanity of English.* Urbana, IL: National Council of Teachers of English.

Britzman, D.P . (1986). Cultural myths in the making of a teacher: Biography and social structure in teacher education. *Harvard Educational Review, 56,* 442-456.

Bruner, J.S. (1962). *On knowing: Essays for the left hand.* Cambridge, MA: Belknap Press of Harvard University.

Bruner, J. S., Oliver, R. R., & Greenfield, P. M. (1966). *Studies in cognitive growth.* New York: John Wiley and Sons.

Clark, C. M., & Peterson, P. L. (1986). Teachers' thought processes. In M.C. Wittrock (Ed.), *Handbook of research on teaching* (pp. 255-296). New York: Macmillan.

Colton, A., & Sparks-Langer, G. (1993). A conceptual framework to guide the development of teacher reflection and decision-making. *Journal of Teacher Education, 44*(1), 45-53.

Conle, C. (1996). Resonance in preservice teacher inquiry. *American Educational Research Journal, 33*(2), 297-325.

Cooper, M. M., & Holzman, M. (1989). *Writing as social action.* Portsmouth, NH: Boynton/Cook.

Craik, F. I. M., & Lockhart, R. B. (1972). Levels of processing: A framework for memory research. *Journal of Verbal Learning and Verbal Behavior, 11,* 671-684.

Danielson, K. E. (1989). The autobiography as language reflection. *Reading Horizons, 29*(4), 257-261.

Elbaz-Luwisch, F. (2002). Writing as inquiry: Storying the teaching self in writing workshops. *Curriculum Inquiry, 32*(4), 403-428.

Emig, J. (1977). Writing as a mode of learning. *College Composition and Communication, 28,* 122-128.

Florio-Ruane, S. (1994). The future teachers' autobiography club: Preparing educators to support language learning in culturally diverse classrooms. *English Education, 26*(1), 52-56.

Fulghum, R. (1995). *From beginning to end.* New York: Ballantine Books.

Gendlin, E. (1978). *Focusing.* New York: Everest House.

Gilyard, K., & Richardson, E. (2001). Students' right to possibility: Basic writing and African American rhetoric. In A. Greenbaum (Ed.), *Insurrections:*

Approaches to resistance in composition studies (37-51). Albany: State University of New York Press.

Hiemstra, R. (1988). Translating personal values and philosophy into practical action. In R. G. Brockett (Ed.), *Ethical issues in adult education* (pp. 19-26). New York: Teachers College Press.

Hiemstra, R. (2001, Summer). Uses and benefits of journal writing. *New Directions for Adult and Continuing Education, 90,* 19-25.

Hollingsworth, S. (1989). Prior beliefs and cognitive change in learning to teach. *American Educational Research Journal, 29*(2), 325-349.

Holt-Reynolds, D. (1992). Personal history-based beliefs as relevant prior knowledge in course work. *American Educational Research Journal, 29*(2), 325-349.

Kagan, D. M. (1992). Professional growth among preservice and beginning teachers. *Review of Educational Research, 62,* 129-169.

Knowles, J. G., & Holt-Reynolds, D. (1991). Shaping pedagogies through personal histories in preservice teacher education. *Teachers College Record, 93*(1), 87-113.

Ladson-Billings, G. (1994). *The dream keepers: Successful teachers of African American children*. San Francisco: Jossey-Bass.

Ladson-Bilings, G. (1995). But that's just good teaching: The case for culturally relevant pedagogy. *Theory into Practice, 34*(3), 159-165.

Lensmire, T., & Satanovsky, I. (1998). Defense of the romantic poet? Writing workshops and voice. *Theory into Practice, 37*(4), 280-288.

Luria, A.R., & Yudovich, F. (1971). *Speech and the development of mental processes in the child*. Baltimore: Penguin.

Mahurt, S.F. (1998). Writing instruction: University learning to first-year teaching. In T. Shanahan, F. V. Rodriguez-Brown, C. Worthman, J. C. Burnison, & A. Cheung (Eds.), *Forty-seventh yearbook of the National Reading Conference* (pp. 542-554). Chicago: National Reading Conference.

Mairs, N. (1994). *Voice lessons*. Boston: Beacon.

McCrary, D. (2005). Represent, representin', representation: The efficacy of hybrid texts in the writing classroom. *Journal of Basic Writing, 24*(2), 72-91.

National Center for Educational Statistics. (2002). *NAEP writing results*. Retrieved December 9, 2006, from http://www.nces.ed.gov/reportcard/writing/results/2002

Norman, K. A., & Spencer, B. H. (2005, Winter). Our lives as writers: Examining preservice teachers' experiences and beliefs about the nature of writing and writing instruction. *Teacher Education Quarterly, 32*(1), 25-40.

Pajares, F. (1992). Teachers' beliefs and educational research: Cleaning up a messy construct. *Review of Educational Research, 62,* 307-332.

Pinar, W. (1994). *Autobiography, politics, and sexuality: Essays in curriculum theory*. New York: Lang.

Progoff, I. (1975). *At a journal workshop*. New York: Dialogue House Library.

Raymond, D., Butt, R., & Townsend, D. (1992). Contexts for teacher development: Insights from teachers' stories. In A. Hargreaves & M. Fullan (Eds.), *Understanding teacher development* (pp. 73-82). Cassell, NY: Teachers' College Press.

Rosenthal, D. B. (1991). A reflective approach to science methods courses for pre-service elementary teachers. *Journal of Science Teacher Education, 2*(1), 1-5.

Rousmaniere, K. (2000). From memory to curriculum. *Teaching Education, 11*(1), 87-98.

Schmidt, P. R. (1996). One teacher's reflections: Implementing multicultural literacy learning. *Equity and Excellence in Education, 29*(2), 20-29.

Schmidt, P. R. (1998). The ABCs of cultural understanding and communication. *Equity and Excellence in Education, 31*((2), 28-38.

Schmidt, P. R. (1999). Know thyself and understand others. *Language Arts, 76*(4), 332-340.

Schon, D. A. (1987). *Educating the reflective practitioner.* San Francisco: Jossey-Bass.

Shields, F. (2002, Winter). Who do we think we are? The ethics and politics of auto-biographical curriculum. *Journal of Curriculum Theorizing, 18*(4), 14-29.

Snyder, T. D., Hoffman, C. M., & Geddes, C. M. (1997). *Digest of education statistics.* Washington, DC: National Center of Education Statistics, Office of Educational Research and Improvement.

Villanueva, V. (1997). Maybe a colony: And still another critique of the comp community. *JAC: A Journal of Composition Theory, 17*(2), 183-190.

Vygotsky, L. S. (1962). *Thought and language* (E. Hanfmann & G. Vakar, Eds. and Trans.). Cambridge, MA: MIT Press. (Original work published 1934)

Willis, A. I., & Hunter, C. D. (in press). Reflective writing: Transforming lives, ideas, and the future of English education. In K. K. Jackson & S. A. Vavra (Eds.), *Closing the gap: English educators address the tensions between teacher preparation and teaching writing in secondary schools.* Charlotte, NC: Information Age.

Yinger, R. (1985). Journal writing as a learning tool. *Volga-Review, 87*(5), 21-33.

CHAPTER 3

THE AUTOBIOGRAPHICAL, REFLECTIVE ASSIGNMENT

Tom Scheft

The previous chapter documented the positive research on having students write about their lives. In this chapter I present an assignment I use with graduate students, and following this, in chapters 4 through 16, are examples by my students and other adults. But this basic assignment can be tailored to students as young as ten years old. I am going to provide the basic steps I use in my educational psychology class, and you will see how this assignment can be adapted to younger students and different academic areas like language arts/English and social studies.

Early in my course, I introduce the assignment in written form:

Studying psychology compels us to think about who we are and how we act. We consider how we are motivated by ourselves and others. Ideally, we journey beyond the textbook jargon and psychobabble to connect with life on a level that is real and meaningful and honest—involving the good, the bad, and the ugly.

Sometimes when we reflect upon ourselves and our lives, it can be overwhelming. In our quest to do more than just make it to the next day, people often have a favorite poem, lyric, quotation, or passage that inspires them—something to turn to for support, for inspiration, for energy when things are

Inspiring Student Writers: Strategies and Examples for Teachers
pp. 31–44
Copyright © 2009 by Information Age Publishing
31

tough. While the words have a significance of their own, the reader's interpretation and relationship with the piece often carry a special noteworthi-
ness.

For this project you are to select a poem, lyric, saying, or passage that is
important to you and explain its significance. Below are several examples
taken from different sources. In each case you'll read a reflective statement
followed by the inspirational piece. Once you've finished the examples, you
should have a clear idea of what I am looking for. However, if you have any
questions, please let me know. You will be turning in your reflective statement and inspirational source (poem, lyric, saying, or excerpt) at the seventh class. I will read and evaluate it. You may be asked to revise it. Actually,
you may be asked to revise your paper several times. Later, you will be
assigned a class period in which to read your piece aloud.

I hope the assignment will be meaningful to you on an individual level,
and I know from past experience it will—quite possibly— allow you to touch
the hearts and minds of your classmates. Additionally, as you explore the
work of your peers, you may want to share some of their works with others.

I then provide several examples—mostly by educators—which typically
talk about the frustrations, the setbacks, the crises, and the victories of
their jobs or other aspects of their lives. The writers talk about losing
themselves, finding themselves. They talk about struggling, about coping.
They talk of failure and success. Here is an example:

I recall a bumper sticker I once saw:

> Life is hard.
> And then you die.

Some people continually look bruised and battered by the struggle we call
"life." You look at them and wonder how they get from one day to the next.
Often they are difficult to be around—their gloom and doom personas
seeming to attach to us, giving off some invisible malaise that saps our
energy. We learn quickly that we'll do almost anything to avoid them.

Other people approach life's trials and tribulations differently. Life is
hard, sure, and there are certainly disappointments and heartaches and
even tragedies to endure. But life is a challenge, not a punishment. Each
day is a new opportunity to prove yourself, to excel, to triumph.

I wasn't too optimistic about life when I first read *A Separate Peace* in high
school. I identified with the struggles of the main character, Gene—his need
to be accepted, his need to find himself, his wrestling with doubts and inse-
curities, his searching for awareness and understanding. It wasn't an easy
book for me. I was a little too "close" to the subject.

Many years later I picked up the novel, and I found new levels of understanding and depth that my adolescent mind hadn't been able to grasp.
Toward the end of the book, there was a short paragraph that suddenly took

on tremendous significance. It was one of those "wow" moments. I read and reread the section several times. Then I stopped and just thought about my life and how it connected so powerfully to this little rectangular block of words.

from *A Separate Peace* by John Knowles [1959]

We reached the beach late in the afternoon. The tide was high and the surf was heavy. I dived in and rode a couple of waves, but they had reached that stage of power in which you could feel the whole strength of the ocean in them. The second wave, as it tore toward the beach with me, spewed me a little ahead of it, encroaching rapidly; suddenly it was immeasurably bigger than I was, it rushed me from the control of gravity and took control of me itself; the wave threw me down in a primitive plunge without a bottom, then there was a bottom, grinding sand, and I skidded onto the shore. The wave hesitated, balanced there, and then hissed back toward the deep water, its tentacles not quite interested enough in me to drag me with it. (p. 46-47)

Now, as I again consider its message, I think: Yeah, life is tough. It is relentless in the problems—big and small—with which it bombards us. But if we are lucky enough, fortunate enough, we react and defend. We are knocked down, but we get back up … over and over. We don't lose our fire, our resolve, our sense of humor. We don't give up. We don't quit. We fight back with a positive spirit. And that helps us appreciate and celebrate the good things. Because so often we do catch the wave … and we ride and ride and ride and ride.

I keep my examples—like the one above—fairly short on purpose. I want my students' first drafts to provide me with some diagnostic information. How skilled are my writers? What are their strengths and weaknesses? How might I help them shape and develop their pieces? I am not expecting the four techniques I mentioned earlier: scene-by-scene construction, description, status life detail, and dialogue. I am not expecting inner thoughts.

What am I expecting? I've been doing this a while (several decades), so I'm expecting pretty tentative, straightforward, lock-step stuff. I'm anticipating the mechanical, monotonic vocal, dutifully following the three-step path:

1. Tell the readers what you plan to tell them.
2. Tell them.
3. Tell them what you just told them.

The first draft usually gives me a sense of how I might make the author a more significant part of the piece, through a specific illustration that uses some or all of the above devices. And after I copyedit the drafts, I also provide some *detailed*, typed feedback. Here is a sample:

> I like your piece very much. [I'll follow this with some specifics as to writing style, use of examples, description, etc.] However, I have an idea for developing it. As such, *I need you to revise this for next class.*
>
> Right now the paper has a general quality to it. You're *telling* us, but you're not *showing* us. You've mentioned the difference you've made in the lives of certain students. That's good, but I want you to add a *specific* example of someone you've helped. Because you'll be writing about a person, here are three strategies to utilize:
>
> 1.   Provide some *brief physical description* of the person, so your readers can formulate a more definite picture in their minds. Doing that personalizes the character for the reader, making him/her a more specific individual than a faceless idea.
>
> 2.   This technique fits nicely with #1. Tom Wolfe, the "new journalist" and author, discusses description in terms of "status life detail." He feels the best illustration gives the reader a sense of a character's socioeconomic status. For example, if someone is wearing a blue button-down shirt, did it come from J.C. Penney or Ralph Lauren? Black loafers—did they come from Pic 'n' Pay or are they Bally shoes (as much as $500 a pair)? Are the sneakers "Air Jordans" (at $150) or K-Mart ($20)? Status life detail can be captured through clothing, hairstyles, material possessions, songs, events, verbal expressions, and/or TV shows.
>
> 3.   Incorporate some *dialogue.* It is a very effective way of establishing an individual and revealing character. Also, readers love to read dialogue. Use it to help illustrate certain scenes.
>
> Example 1:
>   I was angry at how long my 6-year-old son was taking to clean up his room. I told him to straighten his shoes in the closet and then left. When I returned, he was playing on the floor. This time I complained because he hadn't done as I had told him. He quickly ran to the closet, straightened his shoes, smiled, and told me not to be upset. I had to smile.
>
> Example 2:
>   I was angry at how long my 6-year-old son was taking to clean up his room. "Daniel, you're old enough not to have me reminding you every 2 minutes. Now straighten your shoes in the closet."
>   I left the room, but when I returned he was playing on the floor, wearing a Wolverine mask while he smashed two X-Men action figures together in battle. I was furious. "You were told to fix your closet and you haven't. I have a good mind to …'

> Before I could finish, he ran to the closet, straightened his shoes, then wheeled around with a satisfied grin and a mock quizzical look. "I'm sorry, Dad, but what was it you were saying?"
>
> I had to smile. That kid definitely knows how to win me over.

Those are quick examples, but you'll note the difference in involving the reader and establishing the mood and personality. This paper is very good, *but one vivid example can make it better.* Right now you're delivering a strong sense of feeling, but it's not enough. *Show* us what an effective teacher you are. Good luck with the revision.

If it's warranted, I'll schedule a conference. I may also provide specific feedback on writing dialogue or inner thoughts, expanding on an idea, and/or dealing with mechanical or usage concerns. I have all kinds of examples on my computer that I can copy and paste into my comments. For instance, if I want an elementary teacher to convey a better sense of what goes on in her classroom, I'll provide an illustration:

> If a casual observer stuck her head in the door of my classroom, she might instantly wonder: *What's going on in here? Where is the teacher?* You won't see children glued to desks while I lecture. I might be working with a reading group of four students, while my assistant works with another small group on a science experiment—blending colors to make new colors.
>
> In a far corner Janie and Janice look at magazines together, searching for pictures to cut out for a nature collage. In another area, Sean passively strokes his new Carolina blue Nikes, while he listens to a story Shana reads to him. (Later they will draw pictures of their favorite scene from the book and dictate captions to me; I'll write them out, and they will rewrite them on paper and mount them below their pictures.)
>
> Beverly, typically decked out in her favorite pair of jeans and UNC sweatshirt, comes over and politely interrupts me. "Briana, Robert, James, and I want to do a play in the dress-up center. We'll be quiet."
>
> "Okay," I say, adding, "If it's good, maybe some others will want to see it."
>
> "I guess we better make some tickets," she replies.

I have now moved to stage four of the writing process, and we may continue with stages four and five (writing … feedback … revising) for a while.

* * *

One striking aspect of this project is that, typically, students are willing (often after a bit of prodding) to disclose and discuss very personal aspects of themselves and their lives that don't come up in casual conversation. It's surprising.

But it's also not surprising. Writing is a solitary endeavor—just one-on-one with the page or computer screen. Famed sportswriter Walter "Red" Smith once said, "Writing is easy. All you have to do is open up your veins and bleed." Of course he was a man constantly up against deadlines. For the vast majority of my students (and over the years I've taught—literally—thousands), they are *hungry* to express themselves. Despite the difficulty of this task, despite some normal twinge of reluctance, they embrace it—recognizing this "assignment" as more of an *opportunity*.

And when my students read aloud, another bonus is unveiled, which you will see in the student examples. The authors are honest and revealing. Even though we spend a lot of time in education talking about diversity and multiculturalism and tolerance, many teachers don't encourage or require students to communicate who they are.

Fine. Not all classes need to do that. But for those educators committed to breaking down stereotypes and helping students understand and respect each other, what exactly are you doing? Hey, we can build cultural awareness by sharing food and displaying cultural fashions—the popular, fun, easy activities—but when do we really get down to people as individuals?

Thinking stereotypically is a *natural* process. Don't misunderstand. I'm not advocating stereotypical thinking, but if you understand the theory of cognitive psychologist Jean Piaget, that human beings make sense of the world by gathering and arranging information, then you understand how easy it is for humans to stereotype (Piaget, 1954, 1963). We are "wired" to sort/arrange—genetically predisposed to it. Think of the brain as a massive computer hard drive comprised of a plethora of directories and files: food, shelter, transportation, fashion, people, politics, recreation, bad TV shows, religion, travel, leisure, the dumbest songs ever, emotions, and so on and so forth. Take food. Imagine *all* the files and sub-files (pun intended)—from tomatoes to Twinkies to tortillas to tapioca to tenderloin. Consider all the files on people—including cross-categorical references based on personality, religion, race, and ethnicity.

We establish these files (*schemes*, as Piaget dubbed them) at the start of life, at the commencing of thought, and we add to and modify them *constantly* throughout our lives. Sometimes information comes pouring in. Sometimes it trickles in. Sometimes files are bursting with information. Sometimes they are almost barren.

As we seek to understand, a file with little information makes us prone to generalize, to make extreme leaps in logic … often in inaccurate, misleading ways. Here's a favorite example. My son's pediatrician, Dr. R.M. Christian, was a marvelous man with a wonderful bedside manner. Equipped with a warm smile and an ability to make a patient feel cared for and loved, Dr. Christian also happened to be bald. He had such an impact on my son that when 4-year-old Daniel heard the question "What would you like to be when you grow up?", he immediately replied: "A doctor ... a doctor like Dr. Christian." One day, however, after responding to the question, Daniel then asked: "Does that mean I'll have to shave my hair off?"

In the first chapter, I described myself as a 6-year-old living in an affluent, suburban world. Among my many cognitive files was one labeled "Italians." I knew Italians were a different group of people. I knew they spoke English differently from most everybody else. I had some vague notions about Italians being so-named because they came from Italy, which was a place very far away that looked like a boot. I assumed there were female Italians, although I had never met any. And in my 6-year-old wisdom I believed *all* male Italians worked as gardeners.

Theoretically, a scheme filled with information guards against stereotypical leanings. But how much information is necessary to avoid oversimplified thinking? (I delve into this in an appendix chapter, "Confronting Stereotyping: Understanding Why We Do It, Considering What To Do About It.") Life is more complicated than merely setting up categories and filling them with information. After we create a scheme, we begin slipping in new bits of knowledge (*assimilation*, as Piaget calls it). But sometimes we need to alter a scheme. For example, imagine a young child at the zoo looking at a large lion. He overhears an adult say, "That is one big cat." The child has both a cat and a lion scheme, and he finds it humorous that a grown-up doesn't know the difference. He tells this to his parent, who says, "Actually, the lion is a member of the cat family."

Sometimes we can't simply tweak a scheme; we need to develop a new one. Piaget labels the adjustment process as *accommodation*. For instance, picture a child out in the woods who tells his parent he wants to "pet the funny looking cat over there ... the black one with the white stripe down its back." He wants to assimilate this new animal into his cat scheme, but in an instant he's gathered up and whisked off to safety. Once secure, he learns this is not a matter for assimilation; he's got to construct a new scheme: skunks.

Once people think stereotypically, it can be hard to change. Some develop stereotypes early in life and carry them to the grave. However, sometimes—inevitably—we are forced to question a scheme. *We confront an exception.* Piaget describes this state as *disequilibrium*—a condition that may leave us bothered, confused, perplexed, uncomfortable. One response is to *ignore* the exception. In so doing, the stereotype remains.

But in our drive to make sense of the world, ignoring often fails as an option. As much as we'd like to ignore, we *must* confront. In a state of disequilibrium, we seek to restore balance—both emotionally and intellectually. Disequilibrium is a safeguard against stereotyping. Sometimes moving from disequilibrium to equilibration (back to balance, under-standing, awareness) is quick and easy. Sometimes it is lengthy … *extremely* lengthy, to the point of lasting a lifetime.

  Back in the typical classroom, students don't get to know each other beyond superficial levels. Oh, there's idle chitchat and class discussion and sometimes group work or projects, but we don't necessarily know how folks think and feel. The motivational, reflective piece changes that. Semester after semester, my students tell me how enlightened they became about their classmates as *individuals* through the reading aloud of the papers. While diversity and individuality are infused throughout my course, they take on an almost tangible quality through the reflective assignment. Even students choosing the same inspirational source reveal themselves as markedly different, as you will see in three very different papers based on the Langston Hughes poem "Mother to Son." While oth-ers can read the articles for themselves, I've found that authors frequently bring a "little something extra" when reading their work aloud.

A WORD ON VULNERABILITY

While the majority of my students willingly open themselves up to the assignment, for others it is difficult. Each semester, one or two accuse me of violating their privacy. I have been successful at getting those students to relax and accept the task. "I know it's hard," I tell them, "but you're among friends." I also have them read a journal piece former student Brenda Shore wrote for me:

> This assignment of journal writing has been a difficult one for me. I have struggled from the onset, agonizing over the topic to be explored every week. Sometimes, because I did not want to face the internal conflict, I pro-crastinated and left the entry undone, only to be faced with two entries for the next week. Why do I have so much trouble when writing usually comes easily to me?
>
> My first excuse was I did not have anything to say. But, ask any friend or family member and they will tell you I always have an opinion. They will also tell you I love to visit in person and on the phone. So the excuse of nothing to say really does not hold water. So what is the issue?
>
> The issue is … putting my ideas, personal thoughts, opinions in writing for someone else to read. When asked my opinion face-to-face, I can judge the recipient by their facial expressions and body language. Do they really want to know what I think or do they just want confirmation of their own thoughts? I can also choose to open myself up or to hold back, giving only the "safe" answer.
>
> In print, the baring of raw thoughts and opinions is a gamble. Once printed in black and white, there is no turning back. While that little cursor

is blinking, I can erase those lines I have doubts about and those thoughts that are just too personal and hurtful to reveal. But once "print" is clicked, my personal feelings become public, available to anyone who holds this document in his hands. At that point, when you begin to read my thoughts, I become vulnerable.

There. I've identified the crux of the issue: vulnerability. I hate it. I want to have control over all the aspects of my life. I want to hold close those thoughts and ideas that have not been proven, those attempts to apply the information I have learned to my life or the lives of my students. To put them on paper for another to read is to open myself up to criticism and ridicule for not grasping the concepts presented in class, in life.

So be gentle with my attempts to open up, to put onto paper those thoughts I carry in my head. Know that this is a small step in a long journey and you have had a hand in setting me on the right path.

I reassure my reluctant writer/reader that I will indeed "be gentle." I go on to say, "You're not the first person I've asked to trust me on this. I understand your reluctance. I know this is hard, but I have a very good history when it comes to working with students. Nobody has died ... yet. [That usually gets at least a smile.] You will emerge from this remarkably unscathed, and you will be extremely proud of yourself."

*   *   *

Following this chapter are examples. But before you venture there, here's a journal piece by another former student, Nancy Tremalgia, that speaks to many of the points I've raised in this and the first chapter.

One of the things I wanted to get out of this class was a deeper understanding of issues and concepts related to educational psychology, so that I would be better able to communicate my ideas to others. I never imagined it would happen through writing. I absolutely hated writing, and the written reflections have been extremely time consuming and difficult for me. However, going through this process, I became aware of the importance of writing to the thinking process. Writing forced me to think deeper to support my arguments and pointed out areas where I needed to firm up my conceptual understandings.

Even though I have taught creative writing, I did not realize the power of developing academic ideas through writing. I have learned that writing, no matter how painful, seems to force one out of sloppy thinking. It causes one to have to think deeply and critically. My undeveloped ideas were challenged as soon as I saw them on paper. Writing forced me to think through ideas, reflect, and then fine-tune those thoughts. Just taking time to reflect and think seems to be missing from the busy world we live in these days. Giving students a writing assignment as a way to develop and firm up their understanding of freshly learned concepts can be a powerful learning tool. I will now try to incorporate this into my teaching more frequently.

The process of revision is especially powerful to enhance learning. This is where a deeper understanding and a permanent change in knowledge took place for me. I learned this same lesson, but in terms of technical skills, when taking a pottery class at Penland School of the Arts in Spruce Pine, North Carolina. I had made a huge amount of progress under Warren MacKenzie, a master potter from Minnesota. It was inspiring to be in his class; it was like being in heaven for three weeks—no cleaning, no cooking, just total immersion in everything ceramic. All dinner table banter was about pottery, all evening entertainment focused on videos, slideshows, or conversations about pottery and art. We even went on excursions to visit the breathtaking studios of famous potters in and around Penland.

It felt quite different, however, when we moved on to the critique and revision process. I wasn't in heaven anymore. I was in hell. I thought I would die as we went around the table, each person placing their best piece on the table for everyone to scrutinize. Another student, a famous and successful potter herself, was told her piece looked like something you'd buy at Wal-Mart. Warren MacKenzie, whose work focuses on movement and feeling more than technical skill, did not mean this in any way as a compliment.

I started looking for an escape route, but the only one available was crawling under the entire length of the table, and then running out the door. Since that escape method might prove to be even more embarrassing than listening to what he had to say, I stayed put and listened to the other critiques that followed. Each one caused more angst and fear to rise inside me. When he came to my piece, he said, "Well this is an interesting little dish my dog might enjoy eating from if all his other dishes were dirty." I survived this harsh criticism, placating myself with the fact that even the accomplished potters got pretty much the same ruthless treatment.

But that was nothing compared to the revision process. After days of working on perfecting my technical skills—making perfectly straight and tall walls, he strolled by and said, "Nice job, Now let's check to see how straight those walls actually are." I was going to get a compliment from Warren MacKenzie! I couldn't wait for him to bring his ruler over and praise me for the fine job I had done, even if it was just for perfecting my technical skills. I was beaming from ear to ear. He bent down, held the tool perpendicular to the wheel base and said, "Look at that."

Here it was. It was coming, my great compliment from the great Warren MacKenzie, and then he said, "Do you see it?"

I responded with, "Yes, I see it—perfectly straight, tall walls. It has really been worth all the hard work, reclaimed clay, cramped fingers, and sore muscles it took to accomplish this."

"No, don't you see that area with the slight protrusion down near the base. You need to work on that until your piece is completely straight."

What? Improve? I had never seen a straighter-edged vessel in my life. What was he thinking? I couldn't even look. I was just going to wait for him to move on to the next person.

But he didn't leave and go on to the next person, as was his custom. He stayed and silently waited for me to examine my piece. I slowly bent down, not wanting tears to fall over my tall, graceful, straight-walled cylinder. I studied it from all angles, but I couldn't see it. It wasn't there. Surely, he was playing a joke on me. Just as I became convinced that this was an evil trick, I saw it. There it was—a slight, tiny area bowing out near the base of my vessel. I had worked for two solid days to get it just right and I had failed. WHAT A WASTE OF TIME, I kept thinking of the two-day ordeal. WHY DO I NEED TO PAY ATTENTION TO SUCH DETAILS THAT NOBODY WILL NOTICE?

I continued working throughout my three-week stay, and I'm not sure if I ever made a perfectly straight vessel, but I did learn to look for ways to refine my work, no matter how painstaking and long the process might take. In retrospect, I learned the lesson he was leading me to. I see many parallels between this and writing. You perfect your skills and your thinking through thought, revision, and critical examination. Writing exercises a person's thinking muscles, so to speak, like pottery takes physical strength. One goes through a lot of paper, editing and revising as you go, similar to the potter's use of clay. It takes a lot of sleepless nights to figure out how to perfect your written ideas, the same way it takes time and effort to refine technical skills.

It was shortly after my class at Penland that my work began to sell. Many skills converged at the same time, but I believe it had something to do with looking more critically at my work. I feel the process of revising one's written work—looking for a clearer way of explaining an idea, or a better word to more accurately express one's thoughts—leads to deeper and longer lasting understanding.

Nancy's journal entry reinforces a number of salient points. Even teachers who teach writing don't always like to write. Hey, it's hard work; it takes time; it takes effort; and even after that work, time, and effort, your work still may not be *exactly* the way you'd like it to be. The payoff may come later, when we—often grudgingly—look back and *have* to admit: *I'm glad I did that.* Writing is, as she notes, "a powerful learning tool"—different (and often more effective) than thinking or discussing.

She also confirms the value of revision and what can be the positive effects of criticism, but she provides an example in which the artist/teacher's motivation is unbelievably harsh. Hmmmmmm. This is a tricky area, because some people respond wonderfully to extreme criticism (which Nancy eventually did), while others are absolutely immobilized. I worry about teachers who overinflate their students with false notions of their work, but I'm more concerned by the teacher-critics who *shut down* their students.

Educational psychology texts are quick to admonish the harmful effects of "pushing" students, and "experts" will offer "rules" like "never use sarcasm with students." *Really? NEVER do that? Never ever ever?!?!* (Sorry. I'm being sarcastic.) Some of the best teachers I've had—those who really knew me—used all kinds of textbook-no-no's to make me produce at a higher level: public sarcasm, private threats, even hostility. But I had my share of bad teachers who used those *same* techniques—resulting in far different, sometimes disastrous ends.

Nancy's example also relates to a writer's need to be able to stand up to rejection *and get better*—even to the point of getting *great*. I focus on this concern in an appendix chapter, "Helping Student Writers Understand and Deal with Rejection."

If I appear to be "running around" the question of motivation, I'd have to say it's a question that doesn't have a simple answer for me. And rather than expound on that point, I'd like to tell you a little story:

Mr. Goodhue was my seventh grade math teacher—an ornery, old cuss who took off points for *everything*. As a sixth grader, your fear of getting him as your teacher next year was the topic of numerous discussions. It was common practice in his class for a student to get *all* the answers right, yet fail a test or homework. Name in the wrong corner—minus 10. Wrong date—minus five. Rip in the paper—minus 10. No box around the answer—minus 15. You *put* a box around the answer, but it wasn't a very good box—minus 10. Smudge mark—minus five. Another smudge mark—what do you think? Etcetera, etcetera, etcetera.

And then . . . to make it even worse, he turned his students into little Mr. Goodhues. When it came to grading homework, we switched papers and then, diligent members of the Goodhue Gestapo, we ferreted out the culprits. "Mr. Goodhue, doesn't that look like a smudge to you?" "Sir, this doesn't look like a very good box to me."

Benefit of the doubt? R.I.P.

We suffered this day after day after day. Obedient little informers during class, we'd grumble and rail against the unfairness out of class. Finally, one day, one brave soul looked at the big red F on his paper and said what we'd all been saying *outside* of class: "Mr. Goodhue, what is the point of all these stupid, picky deductions for *everything*? What is the point?"

Mr. Goodhue looked at the student. Then his gaze swept across the room. The year was 1961. "Do you know those rocket ships this country is sending into space?" he began. We nodded in unison. He turned to his accuser. "How many parts do think there are in *one* of those rocket ships?"

"A lot, sir."

"Oh, it's considerably more than *a lot*, young man. How many? I'm looking for a number. How many parts?"

"A million. I guess."

Somebody else piped up, "I think there are millions of parts."

Mr. Goodhue nodded. "*Millions* of parts. *Millions* of wires." He paused. There was a very self-satisfied look on his face. He turned back to his accuser. "How much do you think *one* of those rockets costs?"

"Millions of dollars," the student said in a quavering voice.

"*Millions!*" thundered Mr. Goodhue. "Millions and *millions* of dollars. And . . . what happens if just *one* of those wires isn't right? What happens if just *one* of those switches isn't in the right position? What happens if just *one* person hasn't done his job *perfectly*? What happens?"

His accuser said meekly: "It blows up."

"IT BLOWS UP!" bellowed Mr. Goodhue. "Millions and millions of dollars are destroyed, because someone forgot to do something he *should* have done . . . one little thing." He scanned the room. "Sometimes there is no room for just one, little mistake. You have to know the rules. You have to follow the rules. There is no excuse for careless mistakes."

Suddenly, I saw Mr. Goodhue as I'd never seen him before. I realized that his hair was always meticulously in place. He dressed immaculately. While a man in his 60s, he was trim and fit. He was living out his belief.

I'm not sure how many of his students ever "got" the message. It made a big impression on me that day, and it has influenced my life in a variety of ways since then, especially as a teacher.

Now I am a *very* different teacher and person from Mr. Goodhue, but I adapt his message a lot with my students. For example, I talk a great deal about being able to justify *why* you are doing *what* you are doing. As a "child of the '60s," I tell my students to encourage their students to ask why. "And," I continue, "if you can't give them a good reason why you're doing what you're doing, then you ought to *stop* doing it."

CHAPTER SUMMARY

An autobiographical, reflective assignment can easily be tailored for students as young as 10 years old and as old as…. An abundance of research supports the benefits of this kind of assignment.

With this type of writing (or any type of writing), providing examples is very helpful to students and make sure students follow the writing process.

As the teacher, be a helpful, thorough, supportive editor. You can enlist others—parent volunteers, teacher education students, synchronized swimmers, performance artists, rodeo clowns, deposed dictators—but *only* if they are helpful, thorough, supportive editors. *You may have to train them.* Don't assume they have the necessary skills.

Be prepared for student resistance to revision, *but insist on it.* Many students do not understand or appreciate the writing process until *after* they complete the *whole* process.

This writing assignment fits in wonderfully with curricula dealing with multiculturalism and diversity.

REFERENCES

Knowles, J. (1959). *A separate peace.* New York: Scribner.
Piaget, J. (1954). *The construction of reality in the child* (M. Cook, Trans.). New York: Basic Books.
Piaget, J. (1963). *Origins of intelligence in children.* New York: Norton.

CHAPTER 4

TEACHER AS SECRET AGENT

Muri Pugh

Editor's Note: Muri Pugh, a member of the Classics Department at Trinity School of Durham and Chapel Hill, teaches Latin and English grammar, sentence structure, vocabulary, derivatives, translation techniques, and cultural history to young Latin scholars. Muri has been at Trinity since 2005, and is so happy there that she vows to "never leave, just die conjugating verbs in a dead language." In 2006, she was awarded a faculty grant to study differences in learning between the genders based on age-appropriate brain development that has kept her, as her sons would say, "off the street" for the summer. She hopes to incorporate her findings into the curriculum over the next several years to create a more "boy friendly" learning environment.

When she is not teaching or investigating brain development, Pugh enjoys translating seventeenth century English poetry into Latin, or from Latin into English. A "morning person," she literally bounds into Latin class, which has earned her a reputation for being ridiculously perky and addicted to caffeine (neither of which is true).

The following piece was written when Muri worked as an English teacher.

* * *

Inspiring Student Writers: Strategies and Examples for Teachers
pp. 45–50
Copyright © 2009 by Information Age Publishing
45

INTRODUCTION BY SCHEFT

There is a famous/infamous saying attributed to teaching:

Those who can, do.
Those who can't, teach.

Some people add a third line:

And those who can't teach, teach teachers to teach.

Hey, we take a lot of grief, we teachers. Our profession is routinely seen as the "fall-back" option—the second choice … even the "last resort." For some folks it is absolutely mind boggling that people actually grow up wanting to be teachers.

I remember when my son Daniel, a worldly 6-year-old, approached me on the subject. He was—indeed—perplexed. "Do you realize," he questioned, "that teachers don't make very much money?"

I followed with a thoughtful, measured explanation about certain aspects of life being more important than money. I might as well have told the kid: "Blah blah blaaaaaaah … blah blah." If he'd known how to do it, he would have reported me to Social Services.

We've had different versions of this conversation throughout the years, but Daniel's outlook hasn't changed very much. Today, a worldly 22-year-old, he still doesn't fully "get" my choice of occupation, although he's been pretty steadfast in his career plan since age five. Back then it was (and I quote) "big time actor," which brings me to this relevant father-son conversation when he was thirteen:

"Dad, do you think I can be a successful actor when I grow up?"

"Absolutely. No question about it."

"Do you know what I mean by successful?"

"Well … I hope you mean someone who loves to act, someone who really feels fulfilled by acting—whether it's in front of a packed house or just a few people."

He looked at me with that adolescent gaze that says "get real" and "you're lucky parents don't carry permits that can be instantly revoked."

As I think back on that occasion (and others that have followed), I'm struck by the irony of his choice of occupations and his exquisite sense of timing. Once upon a time, back in the Middle Ages, the person who chose to be an actor risked being put to death. And yet—despite that rather extreme deterrent—some people said: "I have GOT to act! It is who I am. I AM an actor. It is why I'm here. Damn the consequences! It is how I must live my life, and I'm going to be the best actor ever."

Imagine the looks they must have gotten from their kids.

* * *

TEACHER AS SECRET AGENT

I teach a core class to general students at a public high school. The students know that they are not in an honor's class or an advanced placement course. Nonetheless, I have high expectations of them. I am willing to work with them to discover creative explanations that help them connect with difficult concepts that elude them. However, often they have decided not to try to master the material before they enter the room on the first day of the new semester.

Some of my students miss class on a regular basis. They have stopped attending school because they do not believe they can complete the credits necessary for graduation. Others come to class and are physically present, but their minds are elsewhere. They sometimes put their heads down and play dead.

I know that I am supposed to be sharing great works of literature with my students, but before I teach them how to read a poem, I have to convince them that they have value. I have to help them see themselves as scholars who are "worth the effort" it takes to learn. Together, we must resist the cumulative effect of their playing dead for years. So, from the moment that I first meet them at my doorway, I affirm them and challenge them to believe they are more capable than they have ever imagined.

Despite the stories they concoct, I accept few excuses. I push them to do their best work because I believe that they are worthy of nothing less. I will not let them quit because they lack a vision of themselves as people who are successful. While I may look like a teacher, I am really a secret agent. My mission is to empower my students, to open their eyes and see the miracles that they are.

When I first met Peyton, I could not tell if she were a boy or a girl. Her clothes were loose and baggy. Her breasts were undefined, and her hair was braided in tight rows that hugged her scalp. She was short and wiry, athletic in build but without the swagger of many of the male athletes I taught. Yet she had an attitude that said, "Don't mess with me." She spoke out in class at inappropriate times; she was excessively loud, but she was always correct. I had no idea where she lived or what her background was. Her clothes gave nothing away. She sported no name brands, insignia, or identifying colors. She wore neither jewelry nor make-up.

Intuitively, I did not "mess with" Peyton, but I suspected her demeanor was a front and that she was less fierce than she pretended. She exuded confidence and a certain air of toughness, but she chose to sit beside a large girl who was obviously pregnant and struggling with the material. Quietly, I watched Peyton pull Shelley through the lessons. She patiently explained the work two and three times when Shelley did not understand. Her only sign of frustration was her tongue tip pushing through the gap between her front teeth when she could not figure out a way to help Shelley grasp the assignment.

Only once that semester did Peyton challenge me. The students were talking about where they were going to spend their spring breaks. Peyton turned to me and said, "How about you, Ms. Pugh? A rich, white bitch like you is probably going to the beach, aren't you?"

I just laughed because the beach is the last place I would go, and I told her, "Peyton, I may be white, but I am not rich or a bitch."

The class stared at me in silent disbelief. I had laughed at Peyton's insult, and said bitch out loud. Still, she persisted. "Well, maybe you're not a bitch, but you're rich, aren't you?"

Shaking my head, I said, "No, I live in a small house. My sons share a bedroom, and I've been wearing these shoes since before you were born."

That seemed to settle things for Peyton. She was more respectful in class and helped Shelley pass the course before her son was born.

After that, I did not see Peyton for several months. She had moved on to the next higher-level course. Unexpectedly, the teacher for that class had surgery, and I was assigned to take her place until she recovered. I noticed Peyton's name on the roll, but I thought there must be a mistake because she was never present. Then, one day she came into class early and handed me a note. "Sign this," she said without making eye contact with me.

I unfolded the note and read the perfect cursive. The note explained that Peyton had been skipping school, signing herself out, and staying home without her mother's knowledge. She had broken her mother's trust, and until she gained it back, she had to have every teacher sign a daily note confirming that she had attended each class.

Without looking up from the note, I asked her, "Is this true?"

"Oh, Ms. Pugh," she said, "I just got so tired of coming to school and working."

"Peyton, Peyton," I said, as my eyes filled with tears, "I know it's hard, but you're smart. You have a chance to do something with your life. You can go to college. You can get out of here and build a better life for yourself. Don't break your mama's heart. She loves you enough to make you be your best self, and so do I."

By this time Peyton was sobbing in my arms. "I know. I know," she said. "If you help me catch up, and I work really hard, do you think I can pass this class?"

"Do you promise me you'll come everyday and give it your best effort?" I asked.

She made me that promise, and I sent her to the restroom to wash her face as the other students filed in and took their seats.

Every day, I signed Peyton's notes. Twice a week, we met after school and went over the material she had missed. Once we had covered those lessons, we continued to meet "just to review," she claimed. By the end of the semester, Peyton had pulled up her grade from an F to a mid-range B. She made an A on the final exam for the course, and went on to take the Advanced Placement class in the fall. Peyton was capable; she just needed to be held accountable by people who loved her enough to see her for who she really was.

The Reason

The reason we don't try harder is that we believe we aren't worth the effort. But what if you *were* the child of God? What if you *were* the light of the world? What if you *could* erase all pain and in place of misery and death, bestow the joy of angels? *Then* would you try a little harder to forgive your neighbor and a little longer to remember your birth in the image of God? If your answer is yes, you just ran out of excuses.

—Hugh Prather

*   *   *

SCHEFT'S RESPONSE

I fell in love with Muri's piece for several reasons. First, there was the "secret agent" metaphor—so clever, so profound. This is no throwaway line. The best teachers are on a mission. For them, the fate of the world does hang in the balance. While they may not be facing off against Dr. No, they're confronting numerous students whose vocabulary seems to consist largely of "No." Like James Bond, these teacher/agents are armed with the most sophisticated weaponry: smiles, hugs, stickers, silence, Skinnerian theory (positive and negative reinforcement, punishment), high expectations, the "look," and—at times—tough words and tough (but appropriate) consequences.

I also loved the metaphor of students "playing dead." We see it all the time. It is maddening, deflating. It is also—as in Muri's case—motivating.

When people say, "I had this one teacher I'll never forget," they are talking about folks like Muri. This piece captures why people make that statement. It also captures why so many people go into teaching and, more importantly, stay in teaching—despite the fact that lot of folks just plain don't get it. I am reminded of the reporter who asked music legend

Louis Armstrong to explain jazz. Armstrong supposedly said, "If you don't know, I can't explain it to you."

And another thing … Muri's tale is an important story that goes far beyond the walls of the classroom. Like the other examples in this book, there are all kinds of hidden ideas and messages, disguised images that are only available to certain readers … even sounds (yes, sounds) that are on uncharted frequencies that only certain readers can hear—which is why at this very moment, while you read these lines, if you stop … and listen … REALLY listen … you will pick up the frantic barking of select dogs going nuts over something in this book. (I may be wrong about some things but not that.)

And even though this is "an educational book" (three words that make me cringe), it is not only that. It is a book of stories. It is a book of magic. It is …

CHAPTER 5

GRATITUDE, GENEROSITY, AND COMMUNITY

Jennifer Lombard

Editor's Note: Jennifer Lombard is a graduate of the Counselor Education Program at North Carolina Central University. She specializes in school counseling and is currently employed as a school counselor at Turrentine Middle School in Burlington, NC. Jennifer has begun presenting at counseling conferences and likes to demonstrate how adolescents dealing with grief can benefit from creative expression. She plans to do additional research in her field. She considers herself an advocate for all children and is committed to working with professionals in schools and communities to help students be successful in school and beyond.

When she is not working, Jennifer loves to spend time with animals, enjoys dining out, baby-sitting, and training for exciting physical challenges—such as climbing volcanoes in Ecuador and participating in small triathlons. She also loves to go on spiritual retreats. Since time is currently a scarce commodity, she can be found looking for "short" ways to contribute to the community—such as donating blood to the Red Cross, biking to work to decrease unnecessary fossil fuel emissions, and smiling warmly at grumpy people. She is also a cosponsor of The Builders Club at her middle school, a service organization for students "to raise money for charities and do other nice things for the community." When her friends ask where she finds the time for her many ventures, she just answers, "Where do you find time to get your money's worth out of that TV?"

This piece was previously published in *The Chapel Hill News*.

Inspiring Student Writers: Strategies and Examples for Teachers
pp. 51–57
Copyright © 2009 by Information Age Publishing
All rights of reproduction in any form reserved.

INTRODUCTION BY SCHEFT

In the course of my career as an educator, I have read 3,457,978 educational "philosophies." Well ... it SEEMS like that many. Except for—maybe—five, they all sounded the same. Everybody loves children. Everybody believes all children can learn. Seventy-three-point-two percent used to teach school to their stuffed animals when they were 3 and 4.

Hey, don't get me wrong. It's important to love children and know everybody can learn. It's fine to name-drop the latest trends and theorists. (Actually, I've got a problem with name-dropping. As a matter of fact, a good friend of mine, Denzel Washington, gets on me about it all the time.)

Here's my question to my students: When somebody reads your philosophy, what will set YOU apart from all the other wanna-get-a-jobbers?

This brings me to Jennifer's piece. She distinguishes herself and adds credibility to her message by mentioning her travels and first-hand experiences in Russia, Hungary, Japan, Yugoslavia, and Ecuador. Note to students: Get out there and travel. Experience this "diversity thing" we call the world.

*   *   *

GRATITUDE, GENEROSITY AND COMMUNITY

*Eat your peas. There are children starving in Bosnia/China/Ethiopia/
Russia/India/and parts of our great country (USA).*

—Famous Motherly Quote

Eating peas won't help the starving children in the world, but there are things we can do to help others. This starts within each person. The lesson for me from the above quote is that we must be grateful for what we have. I hear a lot of people complain in this world. Jobs are too demanding. Gas prices are going up and that fancy car would just make life so much better if only it could be afforded. The house isn't big enough. The furniture isn't quite right. The yard is a mess and it doesn't even have a pool. Morning traffic and the cashier in the grocery store are too slow. Life is a struggle.

When I start to feel this way, I reflect back on the life lessons I have learned through travel, education and development of my spiritual life in order to gain the energy and momentum to go on. When I was 14, I was, like many adolescents, quite concerned about wearing $100 pairs of jeans that came from The Limited Express and having my hair just right. My chief concern was being popular. I wasn't thinking about broader aspects of life, such as having shelter, food, clothes *and* an education.

At this point in my life I traveled with a group of teens and adults to Russia as a citizen ambassador. This was in the winter of 1991-1992 after the collapse of the Soviet Union and at the beginning of an economic crisis that would last 5 years. The shelves in the small grocery stores had little on them. Citizens lived and loved their families in very small apartments, no matter what they did for a living. Freedom of speech was not a given. There was a lot of fear and uncertainty about what the future held. Somehow, designer jeans didn't matter quite so much to me after this experience. Neither did having my hair just right. As for popularity, I realized that true friends didn't care about the external things about me but rather the internal things.

I think about three other trips, each in different parts of the world, that remind me of how incredibly fortunate I am to live and work in the United States. Not that the United States is perfect, but there are so many things I take for granted on a daily basis. Exchange programs to Hungary and Japan taught me that I have a responsibility to facilitate peace whenever possible. From a high hill in Pecs, I could see the rolling hills of the former Yugoslavia just miles away where a civil war raged. In Japan a year later, I attended the annual Peace Ceremony on the anniversary of the dropping of the atomic bomb. The horrors of nuclear war were displayed by objects kept in a museum, such as a piece of stone where the shadow of a person was imprinted upon impact of the bomb, enlarged human organs in jars showing the effects of radiation poisoning, and the charred, twisted remains of children's toys.

My last experience was a 6-month stay in Ecuador, a small country in South America, after my high school graduation. The status of women was much different than in America. Poverty was visible every day and in every way. The lack of public toilets forced the mother of a little girl, perhaps three years old, to help her defecate in the public park. I witnessed a construction worker get hit by a car that was speeding through a neighborhood. No ambulance was called. I am not even sure there were any ambulances. Corruption in the government caused problems and perpetuated the levels of poverty and lack of public services in the country.

I learned through these experiences that very few people have the luxury in which I live. I may be living on a student loan, but I am wealthy compared to most people in the world. I have rights that many people in this world, especially women, can't even dream of having. Small inconveniences in my life take on a different light. My focus has changed to question what I can do to make this world a better place for all people. As I learned about gratitude during the first part of my life, my understanding of my motivation and calling in life has expanded. The United Methodist Church, of which I am a member, has brought a theology of generosity into my life. John Wesley was the leader of the Methodist movement, a movement that began within the Anglican Church in England and dates back to 1729. In addition to spiritual development, Methodists, under Wesley's direction, became leaders in many social justice issues of the day including prison reform and abolitionism. Today, many churches choose to follow his teachings.

Do all the good you can
By all the means you can
And all the ways you can
At all the times you can
To all the people you can
As long as you ever can.
—John Wesley

When I read this quote, I recognize what I have come to understand as my life role, or my calling in life. I struggled with my role in life until September 11, 2001, when I realized my mission is summed up in the above quote. It was three years later that I chose to enter the counselor education program to study school counseling. To remain motivated throughout my career I will need to remember the attitude of gratitude and generosity. A quote from Mother Teresa, another model of generosity, ties my new career path into my current life calling:

Children long for somebody to accept them, to love them, to praise them, to be proud of them. Let us bring the child back to the center of our care and concern. This is the only way the world can survive because our children are the only hope for the future.

I have no idea if I will be able to do anything spectacular for children. Their needs are so great, and my own personal resources of time, talent and money seem so small. I remember the day I met Matthew. The first time I saw the picture of his little infant body in the crib at a rural orphanage in Guatemala, my heart went out to him. He had olive-colored skin and a thick lot of short, jet black hair that stood up on his head.

I began babysitting for his 2-year-old sister just weeks before his arrival. I wished I could afford to adopt children, but I knew that I didn't have the financial or emotional resources to be a parent at that point in my life. But I did need a job, and Mary, their mother, needed a full-time babysitter. I accepted.

One day, shortly after his arrival, Mary asked me to babysit for Matthew so she could spend special time with Elizabeth, his big sister. His curious brown eyes and gentle, toothless grin lit up the room when I arrived. After his mother and sister left, I carried him down the stairs and put him in his Johnny Jump Up seat. As I gazed into his eyes, I had an intuitive feeling that he knew he wouldn't get any more attention and that he was grateful for what he had received. I was not about to leave him, albeit happy, to bounce the morning away while I watched TV for $10 an hour. So I read him "The Big Brown Bear" and "Monkeys Jumping on the Bed." I sang "Twinkle Twinkle Little Star." It was midmorning when I saw him finally realize that I was there just to pay attention to him! The understanding dawned in his eyes and his little face glowed with joy.

Matthew and I have been good buddies ever since. While words were not possible at five months old, at five years old he is nothing but words. The first time I picked him up from kindergarten, I asked him how it was going and he burst into tears and sobbed, "Horrible!"

"Horrible?" I replied. "What happened that made it horrible?"

"I had to turn my card to yellow again and I'm scared to tell mommy 'cause I know she's gonna be SOOOO angry with me!" he wailed.

"What happened? You can always talk to Jennifer about anything. You know that."

"I wasn't following directions and I was talking to Billy."

"Nobody's perfect, Matthew," I replied. "Everyone makes mistakes, even grown-ups."

"Even grown-ups?" He sniffled.

"Yes, and we just try to learn from them and try harder the next time to make a better choice."

These words seemed to calm Matthew down. He chose to tell his mother than night and they worked it out.

Providing children with a safe place to talk and a caring ear for their struggles does plant a seed in their lives that someone has heard their story and has taken time to care for their well-being. Matthew had been scared to face his mother with the disappointing news of his behavior glitch that day, but he was able to talk to me and process his feelings and his problem on the spot. He had a safe and responsible adult who could hear him, advise him and encourage him through his difficulty. Having access to other adults who adhere to the same overall principles but who have different personalities and styles of life can be a huge support to children. And so while I sometimes find myself feeling discouraged when I see the overwhelming needs that exist for many children, I remember that I am part of something bigger, more substantial and far-reaching, like the image reflected in the ancient African proverb:

It takes a village to raise a child.

It is a great honor to be part of the village in my community and help with the bringing up of children in whatever way I can. These themes of gratitude, generosity, the needs of children and the necessity of many people contributing to the lives of children have kept me motivated in the past and will continue to motivate me in the years to come.

* * *

AFTERWORD BY THE AUTHOR

Writing this piece helped me to process consciously and clearly my motivation for entering the counseling profession. When I first considered the assignment, I felt a nagging anger when thinking about entering the educational field because there are so many things I believe are wrong with it. I was also feeling a nagging anger about the state much of the world is in. "Why try?" has been an ongoing question in my life for many years.

As I wrote and revised, I noticed how harsh my words sounded and how protective I felt about my motives. My parents have often cut down my expressions of hope and enthusiasm for helping others, especially through the public schools. They have lost hope and become cynical about many things in the world. Through this project, I was able to consciously process these issues and really look at where I was in my life and my career in a more positive way.

The themes of learning about gratitude, then generosity, and putting those together to work in the community by helping children in schools were both a surprising outcome to my project and yet something I had known for some time. Being able to clarify and express these drives in me will help me be at my best when I am a counselor, because it is a counselor's ethical duty to be self-aware. It will also help me be a better educator, because I will know why I am there. Students will understand my sense of purpose and direction in life, and that will provide a role model for them, because it is easy to lose hope in this world. There will likely be times when I will self-disclose certain things in order to facilitate the counseling relationship. Overall, students will benefit from the clarity I have gained through writing this article.

* * *

SCHEFT'S RESPONSE

Jennifer's piece is effective writing for several reasons:

1. She provides powerful examples—like the gripping artifacts at the Peace Ceremony.

2. The sentences flow well. The word choice is very good. Points are explained and developed well.

     Don't misunderstand. This may sound like I'm "damning with faint praise." Not at all. I consider Jennifer a very powerful writer, but her strength emerges from her calm, straightforward manner. This is something a lot of people don't appreciate, because they think "great" writers use all kinds of stylistic pyrotechnics. Some great writers do. (Tom Wolfe and Shakespeare come to mind.) However, excellent writing comes in many different voices, styles, and formats.

3. While Jennifer evokes lots of visual imagery throughout the paper (like the barren Soviet grocery shelves), it is the Matthew section that adds so much "life" to the piece and really heightens the visual quality. I love the fact that while he is—indeed—a distinct person in his own right, when we listen to his dialogue and his needs, he reminds us of so many other kids the world over. This is one of the great messages of diversity: We are very different; we are very similar. Like the best writers, Jennifer SHOWS this.

     This reminds me of a piece of advice Clyde Edgerton gives to writers: "You don't need to tell your readers everything. Don't underestimate their intelligence. Let them figure some things out."

4. The "gentle, toothless grin" description is a gem. The first time I read that, I had a moment of epiphany. WHAT DID SHE JUST WRITE? I thought. IT IS PERFECT. PERFECT! (I knew I'd be stealing that phrase.)

5. Although this is a very serious piece, Jennifer begins with a humorous tone through the opening quote (a punch line in its own right). She takes a well-worn, clichéd notion (We're lucky to be Americans.) and gives it freshness, emotion, power, and depth.

     As a teacher, when I read student work that is memorable and important, I urge the author to make it available to a bigger audience. Many students politely ignore me—considering my advice the further ravings of a madman. But Jennifer took this to a local newspaper, which eagerly published it.

CHAPTER 6

CONFRONTING
THE FEAR WITHIN

Laura Will

Editor's Note: Laura Will began teaching middle school language arts in her hometown of Durham, North Carolina, in 1998. She and her team received the North Carolina Middle School Association Team of the Year Award in 1994, the same year she became a Teacher of the Year semifinalist for her district. Currently, she is working in the same middle school she attended as a student over 20 years ago, where she serves as a full-time mentor for new teachers. Having recently completed her master's degree in library science at North Carolina Central University, she eventually will return to an instructional position in a classroom or school media center.

When Laura is not teaching, researching, studying, or compulsively buying school supplies, she enjoys various literary pursuits, such as writing song lyrics for her imaginary metal band Rökkähölïckä and composing sarcastic haiku poetry about people who irritate her. She aspires to publish these in an anthology titled *Seventeen Syllables of Snarkasm*. Additionally, Laura spends an inordinate amount of time spoiling her kitty, Schwa, and her rescued pit bull, Stella.

*   *   *

Inspiring Student Writers: Strategies and Examples for Teachers
pp. 59–66
Copyright © 2009 by Information Age Publishing

INTRODUCTION BY SCHEFT

Laura's piece is about facing our fears, and that means making a change. As my friend Pamela likes to say: "The only folks who really like change are wet babies." Change—both good and bad—is stressful.

I have shared Laura's paper with many people—to grab them, to move them, to inspire them to make a change. And so far, it has worked a few minor miracles. With one person, Laura's piece helped her begin therapeutic counseling, on the route to eventually leaving a very bad relationship. With another, Laura's paper helped break the bonds of identity foreclosure. (That's psychology talk for doing what your parents [or others] want you to do, rather than what YOU want to do.) With another, the piece got someone to stop taking drugs and begin facing other concerns.

By the way, this is the original student piece that made me think: WOW. THIS NEEDS TO BE PUBLISHED. I NEED TO PUT THIS IN A BOOK.

So if you have a problem with this book, blame Laura.

* * *

CONFRONTING THE FEAR WITHIN

Like most little girls, I attributed superhuman qualities to my mother when I was a child. Quite literally, I believed she was solely responsible for all things: feast or famine, flood or drought, the phases of the moon. I'd complain to her each time a crescent moon dangled from the heavens, certain that she was the late-night sculptor who had chiseled it down to a banana in the sky. I hoped that if I protested enough, our 1969 Pinto station wagon might fly us to our bumpy destination, whereupon Mama would restore the orb's full, pregnant glory. (These overestimations of my mother's abilities, though imaginative and charming, were rather damaging for both of us, as we've discovered in the years of therapy that have since ensued.)

If my expectations of my mother were unrealistic, I had every reason to believe in her omnipotence. When I was just a few months old, my 25-year-old mother left my father and their lovely but loveless home behind. She set out to begin a new life as a single mother, one in which she would confront and conquer cancer, poverty, heartbreak, and—perhaps worst of all—my adolescent years.

The first lesson I learned in life was that my mother could do anything—change a flat tire, make a lion costume from old pantyhose, install carpet, work a 14-hour day and still read me a story each night. Awestruck, I often would ask her, how? She would stroke my hair, twist one unruly cowlick, and murmur, more to herself than to me, "You must do the thing which you think you cannot do." This was her mantra, her internal prayer for strength, a frequent meditation that, along with black coffee and Salems, propelled her beyond all the barriers this world had to offer. She told me stories about my grandmother—of her survival during the Great Depression, of her giving birth to her first child, my uncle, when she was eighteen years old, while my grandfather was off fighting Hitler in Europe. "Your Mema is a tough lady," my mom has always said. "She's the strongest lady I know." I felt like an impostor among these women. I wasn't like them. They were fearless and invincible, while I was a soft, dreamy, introverted child who cried at the proverbial drop of a hat.

When Mama was busy, I was happiest entertaining myself. Rather than playing with friends my own age, I preferred associating with books, pets, music, crayons, bugs, and food. I spent hours at a time lost in my own idealized fantasy world. By the time I started kindergarten, I had the reading proficiency of a third grader, could write my name in print and in cursive, knew all my numbers up to 20, and could tie my own shoes. I liked the coloring and the counting, the stories and the songs, naptime and snack time. What I didn't like, what I thought I could not do, was talk to other kids. I was well-behaved, but timid, terrified to have been thrust into this fluorescent world of shrieking and chatter. I wanted to go home, to be lost again in my own safe thoughts, to reenter that tiny universe whose only inhabitants were those people I knew and trusted. When I asked Mama to keep me at home so that I wouldn't have to talk to those other kids, she simply sighed, "You must do the thing which you think you cannot do."

Throughout my childhood and adolescence, this was her response to my every complaint, my every fear—ballet, fractions, physical education, exams, men, public speaking, driving, college, work, marriage. She was not unsympathetic; she was, however, a realist, and knew that she could not shelter me from reality, responsibility, hard work, or the threat of failure. In my mind, however, those eleven words had little to do with me.

It was true that I had done many things I thought I could not: I eventually managed an A in math because I stayed after school for help each day until I was sure I understood the concepts. And when I finally overcame my shyness, I was so talkative that my sixth-grade teacher designated a special seat for me in "solitary confinement." By eighth grade, my agoraphobic tendencies had nearly vanished; I joined the drama club, was editor of the yearbook, and hosted a legendary annual Halloween party. Despite those victories, I remained convinced that when it really came down to it, when life started doling out the nitty-gritty, adult-sized problems, I would find that I had not inherited that inner reservoir of courage and fortitude from my mother and grandmother. Ultimately, I would expose myself as a poser, my character lacking the mettle required to be counted in their ranks.

Even so, as I approached adulthood, the words still rang in my head. *You must do the thing which you think you cannot do.* The phrase anchored me whenever I felt fearful—when I ended a disastrous relationship; when I finally stood up to my father; when I worked full-time to pay for college; and, most especially, the first time I stood before of a room filled with teenagers who expected me to teach them something. Like my mother, I unconsciously had internalized Eleanor Roosevelt's oft-quoted phrase, and it hummed within me as automatically as my own pulse. Its presence in my brain did not completely banish feelings of insecurity, doubt, and fear, but it did help diminish their potential to overwhelm or immobilize me completely.

Like Mama, I had my crutches. I avoided the black coffee and Salems, gravitating instead to edible comforts—greasy pizza, rich ice cream, gooey grilled cheese sandwiches, crispy French fries, chewy chocolate-coated caramels. These were my secret indulgences, my rewards for plodding along in this fast-paced world, one in which, since that first shrill day of kindergarten, I was never quite sure I belonged.

And I read. Always willing to abandon my own reality, I consumed books with the same fervor that I consumed calories. Like J. Alfred Prufrock or Walter Mitty, I preferred my own shadowy daydreams to the rigors of the actual world.

It's not that I didn't like my life; I did. I married my college sweetheart and enjoyed close relationships with a loving family and loyal friends. After two uncertain years in the classroom, I was starting to become the kind of teacher I had always wanted to be; my career was truly gratifying. I felt reasonably confident about my ability to work, think, plan, connect, find humor, and communicate in all areas of my life. Professionally and personally satisfied, I had overcome every obstacle in order to achieve the life I wanted—except for one.

Throughout my life, my tendency to hide myself from the outside world had physically manifested itself in pounds and pounds of extra flesh. Bite by bite, without even realizing it, I had managed to stow away my inner self in a cocoon of fat. The words that described my body became more ominous as I grew older—*plump* at age 8, *buxom* at 18, and, finally, at age 30, the clinically brutal *morbidly obese*. My 5-foot frame carried more than 130 excess pounds. To my friends, family, husband, and students, it seemed to be a nonissue. My large body was merely an extension of my personality; I was jolly and exuberant, and well loved for it.

Even then, I vaguely understood that I was ignoring the truth that hung plainly from my hefty hips. Once again, I believed I was the weak link. Of the strong, disciplined, tireless matriarchs in my family, I had been the one to fail, the one who quite clearly could not fulfill the promise of doing that which I thought I could not do. I could live with the physical sensation of being fat. I found some comfort in it, actually. However, I no longer could live with my own personal weakness or with the notion that it was on display for everyone—especially my students—to witness. I became determined to lose the weight.

When I resolved to act, the strength was there, waiting, as it had been all along. I ate healthfully and made time for daily exercise. After losing the first 50 pounds, I joined a gym where I worked out several times a week. I gave up the habits that had given me a false sense of safety for so long, opting instead to battle the insecurity that spawned them. Eighteen months later, when I was 125 pounds lighter, it became clear to me that I *do* possess the strength of my mother and grandmother. Indeed, I was never without it. That strength resides within everyone, where it remains hidden until you have the courage to call upon it. And when you accomplish the task you perceive as impossible, when you "do the thing you think you cannot do," only then do you liberate yourself from fear, making it possible to pursue the life you really want.

My newly acquired sense of empowerment has nothing to do with the number on the scale or the labels on my new clothes. It has nothing to do with my appearance. (In fact, I remained critically doubtful of my strange new reflection in the mirror.) The freedom I experienced transcended the physical aspects of weight loss. It was a fulfillment unachievable via superficial or external means. Rather, it came from triumphing over the most daunting inner demons, transforming fear into personal power.

Surely, Eleanor Roosevelt had no idea that her words would be hijacked by multiple generations of mule-minded Southern women possessing the wits and determination to live them out. Last year, I saw the quotation in its entirety for the first time, emblazoned on an overpriced magnet in a floral-scented gift shop:

> You gain strength, courage, and confidence by every experience in which you really stop to look fear in the face. You must do the thing which you think you cannot do.

As I have yet to overcome my compulsive shopping disorder, I bought three of them.

* * *

SCHEFT'S RESPONSE

When I first read Laura's piece, I was struck by the quality of her writing—especially the wit and depth of feeling. I had NOT noticed that in her class discussion, and this speaks to a "bonus" writing provides. Often when we write, we open up on the page in ways we would never dream of or dare to when speaking. This is one reason I use journal writing in all my classes. Journaling helps people write honestly about things that matter to them. Then, when it's time to write that "formal paper," students aren't panicked and wondering, WHAT CAN I POSSIBLY DO? They've developed a number of good ideas, real ideas, important concerns from which to choose.

One technique Laura's piece illustrates is the writer making herself vulnerable to the reader. It is so hard for many of us to admit to our mistakes, to reveal our shortcomings. I've known too many educators who believe it is "wrong" to acknowledge their errors, ESPECIALLY in front of students. "You undermine your authority," they warn. "You damage your credibility."

I totally disagree. And I like the strategy of those educators who PURPOSELY reveal they do NOT know everything, establishing early (and often) to their students that it's NORMAL and FINE to make mistakes; it's important to correct them; and there are all kinds of ways to find answers—without assuming that one must know everything.

We often fear making ourselves vulnerable, because when we do … well, then we're vulnerable, and who wants that? We also lose some control. And who wants that? But writers who make themselves vulnerable help their audience relax their defenses—allowing them to confront their problems and limitations, to open up, to share, and—often—to heal. Writers willing to do this emerge as very strong individuals—serving as a source of strength to others, connecting on an immediate, personal level. SOMEBODY UNDERSTANDS ME, thinks the reader. I'M NOT ALONE. And in some cases this allows the reader to think: MAYBE I'M NOT SO STRANGE, WEIRD, BAD (ALL OF THE ABOVE) AFTER ALL.

I again return to the "power of print." Conversation can certainly be motivating and life-altering, but conversation is easily interrupted. Depending on our state of mind, we may be distracted—taking in the words but focusing on something else, someone else. Print is different. We are forced to engage—to look at the words. If we wander, it's pretty evident, and we are aware of our need to refocus.

Another advantage of print is our ability to craft language. Laura—the author, an extremely bright person—doesn't normally speak like this paper. And while some say that writing is merely "talk written down," and while it can sometimes be that, it is not always that, and it is not always that simple.

Writing is an art form. With the English language we have a basic set of tools, nine patterns of language with which to communicate:

1. Subject-Verb:
    Billy runs.
2. Subject-Verb-Direct Object:
    Harriet eats strawberries.
3. S-V-Predicate Adjective:
    Strawberries are good.
    or
    Predicate Nominative:
    Sally is the president.
4. S-V-Indirect Object-DO:
    Harriet gave her brother a strawberry.
5. Expletive:
    There is Andrea.
    It is Andrea's job.
6. S-V-DO-Objective Comp.:
    We elected Sally president.
7. Question:
    Where is John?
8. Passive:
    The strawberries were eaten by Harriet.
9. Command:
    Come here, John.

Despite that small number of patterns, by compounding and subordinating them, we can create an INFINITE variety of sentences. Through our choice of words, we can find better ways to communicate, to make clear, to illustrate, to dazzle. Let's revisit Laura's opening paragraph:

> Like most little girls, I attributed super-human qualities to my mother when I was a child. Quite literally, I believed she was solely responsible for all things: feast or famine, flood or drought, the phases of the moon. I'd complain to her each time a crescent moon dangled from the heavens, certain that she was the late-night sculptor who had chiseled it down to a banana in the sky. I hoped that if I protested enough, our 1969 Pinto station wagon might fly us to our bumpy destination, whereupon Mama would restore the orb's full, pregnant glory. (These overestimations of my mother's abilities, though imaginative and charming, were rather damaging for both of us, as we've discovered in the years of therapy that have since ensued.)

Now ... imagine Laura is standing before you, and you say, "Tell me about your mother." Do you expect those SAME words in the SAME order to come out of Laura's mouth?

If you can produce well-crafted writing, you have got some serious power.

CHAPTER 7

TEACHER AS SCIENTIST, TEACHER AS ARTIST

Amanda Albert

Editor's Note: Amanda Albert is a graduate student earning a degree in Communication Disorders at North Carolina Central University. She aspires to become a speech therapist, aiding young students with speech/language difficulties while "playing games all day long." Currently working in a self-contained elementary classroom, her novice intuitions and adaptive strategies are frequently implemented into classroom operations. Amanda's "anal" organizational demands bolster the efficiency of fellow educators and the successes of her young learners. Her outspoken observations and willingness to "try ANYTHING" incite highly experienced colleagues to reevaluate procedures and purposes of personal and professional philosophies.

When Amanda's not working one of two jobs, sweating in class at NCCU, or typing away at the computer, she has her hands in the dirt of her garden, which, in its first year, was "limping to the tune of its demise," no thanks to the relentless scorching of North Carolina sun fire. This year, she decided to plant cacti and forget about it.

Inside her head, thoughts are constantly being translated from English into Thai, Polish, and/or Spanish. Since her fluency with all three is limited to conversational, the results consist of an intermingling of words from all three languages that "god, allah, buddha, madka earth, and padre sky" know only Amanda could possibly accept as meaningful.

* * *

Inspiring Student Writers: Strategies and Examples for Teachers
pp. 67–74

INTRODUCTION BY SCHEFT

Here's a little tease. When I read the last sentence of this piece, I froze. I read it again. I read it several more times. WOW, I kept thinking to myself. WOW. WOW. WOW.

* * *

TEACHER AS SCIENTIST, TEACHER AS ARTIST

From *The Story of My Life* by Helen Keller

Someone was drawing water and my teacher placed my hand under the spout. As the cool stream gushed over one hand she spelled into the other the word water, first slowly, then rapidly. I stood still, my whole attention fixed upon the motions of her fingers. Suddenly, I felt a misty consciousness as of something forgotten—a thrill of returning thought; and somehow the mystery of language was revealed to me. I knew then that "w-a-t-e-r" meant the wonderful cool something that was flowing over my hand. That living word awakened my soul, gave it light, hope, joy, set it free!

I was nearly 7 years old, the same age as Helen Keller in the passage above, when I first discovered its uniqueness. How strange it was to have such a view into a life so different from my own, and revealing so clearly that other minds could be so different from mine. My childhood was ordinary enough for me to assume that the thoughts and experiences of others must be much like my own. That difference was a revelation for me.

In the same way that the flowing water made the concept of language a reality for Helen, the words of her story make the vast gulf that can separate one mind from another a reality for me. Often throughout my life, I imagine the teacher's fingers spelling out each letter of the word w-a-t-e-r, patiently and persistently building a bridge to reach out across that gulf. Eventually, I came to know that I could do that as well, and have consciously sought to emulate Sullivan's style as an educator.

My greatest "Aha!" moment occurred with an apparent nonverbal, African American, 5-year-old boy with big chocolate hazy eyes and splotchy, scabbed, insect bitten, cocoa skin. I spent 2 months, working one-on-one with him, focusing on weakening his negative behavior through redirection and definition of school expectations, while the resource team conducted assessments and met frequently trying to determine and justify his least restrictive environment placement. I implemented a sticker reward system that allowed him to choose activities with which he would succeed, offering incentives such as time with Spider, a 12-inch, hairy stuffed spider with eight malleable legs. Markus began to use his words and respond appropriately to adult requests.

Markus's first full day in the special education class was one of the loneliest moments in my life. Resuming the neglected schedule of the past two months, I questioned my purpose. One morning, I heard Markus screaming as I approached his class. I entered to discover an assistant struggling with a student while Markus was curled under a table, with the look of death in his eyes. After being made aware that his expected task was writing, I asked, "What does your schedule say?" Ignored, I said, "Ok, if you write three sentences, Miss Albert will bring Spider to eat lunch with us."

He immediately came out, moving toward the writing center. "Let's write about Spider," I responded, continuing to prompt his writing.

Markus proceeded to sound out each letter, of each word, for each of his three magnificently designed sentences. He got a well-deserved sticker and a hug before I left to retrieve Spider joyously. We all ate lunch together, peacefully, that day.

I strive daily to be creative, imaginative, eclectic, adaptive, and experimental—employing whatever resources are literally at hand, so as to shape the key to the lock of understanding ... not to be just the hand that spells the word, but to be like the water in the hand.

* * *

AFTERWORD BY THE AUTHOR

While writing this piece, I was overcome by feelings that defined my moments with Markus as revolutionary. My heart raced as the words poured from my fingertips, hoping that the speed of transmission from heart to paper would not forsake the power of our interactions. The longing to be with Markus resurfaced, forcing me—then a fledgling "educator"—to reevaluate my short, powerful month with him.

I am still wondering what this all means. At the start, I wasn't sure if I could do the job, and as someone who likes to be sure, who NEEDS to be sure, I was nervous. I was the "new kid" at the school, one without formal training, uncertain of what I was bringing, uncertain of what the veteran teachers wanted me to do. I believe all they were looking for was a "warm body," someone to baby-sit Markus while they figured out what to do with him. That role was not enough for me. I had to do more, and through that belief and my normal, intense work ethic, I came to find an abundance of talents. Now, after several semesters of formal training in a university setting, I realize I didn't need many of the advanced, formal skills taught to aspiring special educators. I just needed to connect with Markus on a very basic level—with very human, immediate communication.

I was nervous when I first met Markus. My superiors defined my daily responsibilities as solely "to be" with him. I recall my determination to prove my professional abilities and, more importantly, to take this assignment for what it could be: an invaluable opportunity to discover myself, as well as reach him.

I once heard a teacher say, "Students come to us where they are." That seems like an obvious statement, but it's complicated. There are developmental concerns, social issues, physiological matters, morality factors, skill factors, and other things we may have no clue about. This is what makes teaching so hard. You're trying to assemble this puzzle, but some times—many times—you never get to finish.

Students come to us, and they want/need something. Most are willing to work for it. As educators, we come with our bag of incentives and tricks; we're ready to lead the child. We like to control the situation. But what happens when that doesn't work? Trust me: It doesn't often work with special education children.

With Markus, I decided almost immediately to let him lead. I spent a good bit of time just talking with him, trying to "learn" him, trying to get a sense of what motivated him. These interactions were very basic, very fundamental—classic stimulus and response. What was his "safe zone"? How far would he let me in? To what extent could I push the limits?

Why was I so nervous to be with one 5-year-old boy? He was coming from a home in which he was neglected. He was coming with fear. His behavior was alternately combative and passive. I was coming from another world, a vastly different childhood. I was raised to be independent. I was supported in my home. I had no fear. That was part of my family. "Just try it out," my parents would often say, and that was one of the many positive messages I remember from my childhood. I'm not even sure people in his family talked very much to Markus.

He had to survive. He had to fight for attention, and probably was desperate enough to try most anything. What must he have felt about adults, especially those closest to him? What had he learned from home? As I tried working with him, I could imagine him thinking, SHE JUST TOLD ME TO DO IT AGAIN. MAYBE IF I IGNORE HER, LIKE I DO EVERYBODY ELSE, SHE'LL STOP BOTHERING ME AND GO AWAY.

There was so much I didn't know ... yet. He did not know how to express his willingness to work, and maybe that kept him from knowing what to do, how to begin. And I—initially unaware—felt responsible to meet his needs during our time together.

The forces of Maslow's hierarchy challenged our success. Until basic needs of safety and belonging are met, says the theory, certain learning can't take place. This premise disguised Markus as being more unreachable than I discovered him to be. Most of our days were spent alone together. We created our own comfort zone where limits, which had been conceived by others to keep Markus reined in, were redefined. Actually, we didn't just redefine them. We kicked some of them down.

For example, instead of NOT allowing Markus to go outside (because others feared he might run away or not return in an orderly manner), I decided to use going outdoors as a reward. I'd enlist the support of another teacher to join me outside for 10 minutes on the basketball court. I needed Markus to respond and comply when working or playing. While I was, to some degree, bucking the system, I also needed to fit into the system—to be perceived as a valued part of the team, not some radical, what-the-hell-is-she-doing threat.

We continued to work at creating our own freedom, with certain limits still in place. He changed. He no longer sat zombie-like, unresponsive, doing nothing besides dropping his pencil, tuning out. This is a part of working with exceptional children many don't understand. In the past, getting Markus "on task" for two minutes was out of the question. A minute? Forget it. But that started to change. We found our way to enlightenment in each other. Eventually he could work for 10 minutes at a time. And it was more than my telling Markus what to do ("Point to the square.") and his merely complying. He grew out of his pattern of not cooperating. I could give him two- and three-step directions ("Markus, I'll know you're ready when you pick up your pencil and write your name.") without additional prompting, and he would take over. This was quite an achievement—especially for some of Markus's former teachers, who never considered this result in their wildest dreams.

And what was my magical, mystical strategy? Talking. And listening. Trusting. Positive reinforcement. Was it really that simple? Yes ... and no.

In hindsight, I realize the low expectations placed on him by some in the Exceptional Children's Department shook me. They—the veterans, the professionals—didn't know what to do with this child beyond containing him.

Don't misunderstand. This is not a piece about heroes and villains. Most great teachers I know have stories—several stories—of students they "failed," opportunities lost, squandered, and misconstrued. Sometimes we get lucky. Things work, and we are pretty certain why. Sometimes they don't. We shrug our shoulders and move on. Or we agonize and beat ourselves up—again and again and again. Being a special educator can be a crazy-making profession.

In the beginning with Markus, I didn't know the strength of my position. I didn't know my power. I didn't know the difference between my power to control and my power to inspire.

I do now.

* * *

SCHEFT'S RESPONSE

When I worked with Amanda on her afterword, we went through several sessions. She wanted to explain things clearly, and sometimes it took a little while—a chance to stop, get away, think, and come back again for another try. Conversations would sound like this:

Amanda [*pointing to a sentence*]: This made sense when I wrote it, but it doesn't sound right now.

Me: How about this? [*I'd scribble something.*]

A: No. Not really.

Me: How about THIS? [*I'd scribble something.*]

A: Ummm. No … but better. What about … [*She'd scribble something.*]

Me: Ah! Good. But explain this part to me …

We were between revision sessions when I read an article by Barbara Bartholomew (2008) and immediately thought of Amanda's afterword:

> As a new teacher, I had assumed what most in the field of education believe to be true: motivation springs from effective curriculum and instruction. If we have some perfect blend of elements—direct instruction, whole-language instruction, a new trade book or textbook, an intervention, a new set of standards—students will become deeply involved and interested learners. Everything circled back to effective curriculum and instruction. It had been the focus of my college course work, of every professional developments session I had ever attended, and of every piece of advice I had ever received from a principal. But it was clear to me from that first experience that the most vexing issues I faced as a teacher stemmed less from the content that I knew and control than from the context of things I didn't know and could not control.
>
> Chief among these things was what made my students tick. Human thought processes are not directly observable. Because we see others behaving in a way that is consistent with our efforts to influence their actions, we deduce that we have succeeded in our attempts to motivate them. But for every teacher who has run a "token" society, rewarded those who comply with candy, phoned a parent to gain a student's cooperation, changed seating charts in the hope of ending chatter, or flashed classroom lights as a signal for silence, it remains unclear exactly what is motivating the students. It is easy to confuse behavioral cueing with motivational change. (p. 141)

That passage helps explain why I refer to teaching as a science and an art.

Revisit with me the last sentence of Amanda's piece:

I strive daily to be creative, imaginative, eclectic, adaptive, and experimental—employing whatever resources are literally at hand, so as to shape the key to the lock of understanding ... *not to be just the hand that spells the word, but to be like the water in the hand.* (italics added)

Whew.

We talk a lot in education about the power of expectation. It is frightening—for both good and bad reasons. For example, there is the famous self-fulfilling prophecy—a concept many people THINK they understand, but they don't. Many define it as "something that comes true because you expect it to." Nope. Borne of the controversial research of Robert Rosenthal and Lenore Jacobson in the mid-1960s, the self-fulfilling prophecy is a FALSE or GROUNDLESS expectation that leads to behaviors that bring about the original expectation, making it "true" (Merton, 1948). Research indicates that students live up or down to the expectations of teachers. Of course it's not limited to teachers and students. All of us are susceptible to the expectations of others.

High expectations. Well ... okay. I know lots of excellent teachers who purposely plant these and reap positive results. Negative expectations, however, can lead to skirmishes ... then battles ... then wars. As people "live down" to certain expectations, they dig themselves into holes ... and keep digging.

Self-fulfilling prophecies are going on all around us—24/7 ... 365. Somewhere in the world, a star halfback is out for the season with a broken bone, but a coach is filling a back-up player with massive doses of hype, all manner of phony praise and promise. And that second-stringer, that kid who'd gotten used to riding the bench, he starts drinking protein shakes, getting up at 5 a.m. to lift weights, staying after practice to work on his moves. And maybe he won't replace the star. But maybe, just maybe, he will.

Years ago, there was an urban myth that a popular chewing gum had spider eggs in it. Sales of the gum plummeted.

By the way, reading this book ... Wait a minute ... BUYING this book and then reading it will help you lose weight, increase your intellect, and make you better looking. Honest. Hey, have I lied to you?

Try this expectation: ALL our students are writers. They all have stories. They all have something to say.

Some don't need our help very much. We need to get out of their way.

But some do need our help ... and our encouragement ... and our guidance. They need all those things, and they need them a lot.

Let me sum this up in the words of a retired school administrator, former middle grades and high school teacher, lecturer, consultant, and master storyteller, Dr. Dudley Flood:

We don't always know who our students are. Our students don't always know who they are. But our students often become who *they* think *we* think they are.

REFERENCES

Bartholomew, B. (2008). Why we can't always get what we want. In *Annual editions: Educational psychology*, (23rd ed., pp. 141-145). Boston: McGraw Hill.

Jussim, L., & Eccles, J. (1995). Naturally occurring interpersonal expectancies. In N. Eisenberg (Ed.), *Social development: Review of personality and social psychology* (Vol. 15, pp. 74-108). Thousand Oaks, CA: SAGE.

Merton, R. K. (1948). The self-fulfilling prophecy. *Antioch Review, 8*, 193-210.

Wigfield, A., & Harold, R. (1992). Teacher beliefs and children's achievement self-perceptions: A developmental perspective. In D. Schunk & J. Meece (Eds.), *Student perceptions in the classroom* (pp. 95-121). Hillsdale, NJ: Erlbaum.

CHAPTER 8

REFLECTIONS ON LANGSTON HUGHES' "MOTHER TO SON"

Casey Collins, Carron Carter, and Melissa Davis

INTRODUCTION BY SCHEFT

This chapter includes three pieces inspired by Langston Hughes' famous poem, "Mother to Son," a poem widely anthologized and used by numerous educators. I don't recall how many times in my life when reading a passage or a poem took my breath away, but that happened with this poem decades ago, and I still feel its message today every time I read or hear it—this work both timeless and universal. I find it daunting and inspiring. Remembering those who suffered and fought and marched and endured and even died for me, for us, is a humbling, troubling, uncomfortable, yet ultimately motivating experience. It pushes me to work hard, to strive. I know it has, and will continue to have, this same effect on millions and millions and millions of people.

Inspiring Student Writers: Strategies and Examples for Teachers
pp. 75–86
Copyright © 2009 by Information Age Publishing

75

MOTHER TO SON

Well, son. I'll tell you:
Life for me ain't been no crystal stair.
It's had tacks in it.
And splinters.
And boards torn up.
And places with no carpet on the floor—
Bare.
But all the time
I'se been a-climbin' on.
And reachin' landin's.
And turnin' corners.
And sometimes goin' in the dark
Where there ain't been no light.
So boy, don't you turn back.
Don't you set down on the steps
'Cause you finds it's kinder hard.
Don't you fall now—
For I'se still goin', honey.
I'se still climbin',
And life for me ain't been no crystal stair.

—Langston Hughes

* * *

Editor's Note: Casey Collins, a third-year physical education teacher at Mt. Vernon Middle School in Raleigh, N.C., recently earned her master's of physical education from North Carolina Central University. She also works part-time at Communities in Schools, an after-school tutorial program for children K-12. "We serve children from low-income communities and try to get them motivated to do their homework and stay out of trouble," she said.

"As for free time," says Casey, "I don't have much, but I love to play with my puppy, attend basketball games, and watch the Lifetime Channel. I'm also mentoring a 16-year-old woman. She's an athlete, and we work on her soccer skills."

* * *

REFLECTIONS ON LANGSTON HUGHES' "MOTHER TO SON"

It's funny how a poem, adage, or proverb can mean a thousand words to someone who's experienced what the author writes. However, to someone else it's just another publication. Maybe "Mother to Son" by Langston

Hughes was a good-to-read poem for you, but to me … it foretold my life story.

Imagine a little girl dressed in baggy pants that used to be her brother's, a dingy T-shirt, and white and blue shoes that spelled Wal-Mart to the kids at school. She lacked confidence because she didn't have the trendy clothes or shoes that her friends wore. Her hair reeked of oils because her mom didn't want her curl to look dry. Growing up in a low socioeconomic status, single-parent household with two other siblings was definitely not my idea of a crystal stair. There were times when my mother struggled to put food on the table, and the now disgusting Ramen noodles posed as my steak or chicken today. There were times when I didn't want to stand in the welfare line to get peanut butter and cheese, but I had to—if I wanted to eat. There were also times I wished for a fatherly figure who could help us through the hard times, but he didn't. He only made it worse.

My stepfather definitely symbolized the tacks, the splinters, and the torn up boards that Hughes described throughout his poem. Before the marriage, he was 6'1", 170 pounds with muscles and an afro. He was a very nice looking gentleman. A year or two after the marriage, he was still 6'1", but he had gained weight. He had put on 60 to 70 pounds and his breath reeked daily of alcohol. I think it was the combination of the drugs and alcohol that made him turn evil.

He would always come into the house with this angry look on his face, as if the world had done him wrong. I don't ever remember him saying "hey" or kissing my mom. He would go into their room, take a shower, and lie in bed until my mom took him dinner.

Dinner was never good enough for him. "Barbara, this food is not warm. It's not done enough. It's not good. Fix me something else!"

For a long time my mom would fix him some more food, but I guess one day she got tired. "I'm not fixing any more food!"

I couldn't believe it! My mom finally stood up for herself.

Then the beatings began. I heard a loud scream and my mother say, "Stop. You're hurting me."

I laid down on the couch and cried because I couldn't do anything. My oldest brother was off at Job Core and my other brother was just as scared as I was. That night we waited for our mother to come out of the room and let us know that she was okay. She never did … until the next day.

After that night things got worse. My stepfather became more abusive (physically and mentally), discouraging, angry, and jealous.

But all the time I'se been a-climbin

I've looked past the way people have treated me, the fear that my stepfather instilled in me, and the smirks I've received when I've told people that I was going to succeed.

I remember the day that I tried out for the middle school basketball team. I didn't have many friends and if my memory serves me right, I could only dribble. A couple of the eighth grade girls and my stepfather saw fit to tell me that I would never make the team.

"You're gonna be just like your mom—pregnant at 17 and working in a factory for the rest of your life. You'll never be anything. You'll never get out of Tarboro."

Those words ran through my mind constantly. I fought to prove him and those girls wrong. I studied harder than the average kid. I practiced twice as hard and longer than the other girls.

As I look back on everything that has happened to me and at the lack of accomplishments of my critics, I wonder how they felt when they found out that I was going to college. I wonder how they felt when they heard I had a scholarship to play basketball. I wonder how they feel now that I am an educated Black woman who's seeking to attain a masters.

> *So boy, don't you turn back.*
> *Don't you set down on the steps*
> *'Cause you finds it's kinder hard.*

My life story is truly my inspiration to teach. I seek not only to fill the students with knowledge, but also to provide them with a mentor, one who will inspire in them the everlasting hope to which "Mother to Son" alludes.

* * *

SCHEFT'S RESPONSE

While certainly a triumphant story, Casey's tale is a bittersweet one for me, reminding me of so many students—too many students—who have shared a similar childhood. While most of my students at NCCU are those who have avoided and/or risen above tragedy, they typically have first-hand stories of many children who didn't.

From a technical standpoint, Casey's paper offers the reader wonderful bits of description and status-life detail that lead to clear visual images: the Ramen noodles, the welfare line for peanut butter and cheese. The stepfather is a flat character, a shadowy figure, but that works in this context. He doesn't deserve elaboration and attention beyond the brief physical characteristics Casey provides. The once "very nice looking gentleman" has—literally and figuratively—let himself go, "turn[ed] evil." Some characters do not require much detail, but they need some. Otherwise readers struggle unnecessarily to create the scene in their minds.

*   *   *

Editor's Note: Carron Carter, a media specialist at West Lake Middle School in the Wake County Public School System, teaches media studies and information literacy. "This is where I belong," says Carron, who began her career as a social studies/language arts teacher "a hundred years ago." Along the way she had children, became a trailing spouse as her husband climbed the corporate ladder, returned to teaching 14 years ago as an in-school suspension teacher, and then decided on a new career path in spring 2002. Carron graduated summa cum laude from the NCCU School of Library Science in December 2005 to the delight of family and friends. She hopes that eventually she will find the time to read for pleasure again and travel during those long summer vacations she hears that teachers have. Her current challenge is the quest for National Board Certification.

*   *   *

The poem by Langston Hughes, "Mother to Son," transcends time, race and gender and is just as poignant today as a motivational tool for my students and me as when it was first published decades ago. If my father had been a poet, he might have spoken to me as this mom did to her son about the fact that she had been given no crystal stairs. He would have told me of the challenges that he faced as the son of an unsuccessful sharecropper, grade school drop out, World War II veteran, and how hard it was to continue as a barber after nearly cutting his hand off.

While remodeling his barbershop he accidentally dropped a mirror—cutting through his wrist and the bone of his left arm. His arm was surgically repaired but his hand was never the same again. I remember the weeks of hospitalization, the agony he went through during the healing process, and the way his hand withered. As soon as he came home from the hospital, he got up every morning, put on a starched, long sleeve white shirt, tie, pressed pants, shinned shoes, and, after making sure that every red hair was correctly in place, went to the barbershop. He was and still is a feisty little man, standing less than 5'6" on skinny, little bird legs. He always wanted to look his best, and while his clothing wasn't from the most expensive stores in Birmingham, they definitely weren't from Sears or Penney's either. He wanted the trappings of middle class success even during the dark days of his recovery without medical or disability insurance.

It was months before he could cut hair again, but it didn't matter. He was at the shop every day doing whatever he could do. It couldn't have been easy to teach himself to cut hair without the use of his left hand but he managed. In his later years, he managed to become the owner of two barbershops, an instructor in his own barber college, and an internationally known judge in men's hairstyling. At the age of 80, he is still cutting hair 2 days a week.

He was not an eloquent man, but he taught me by the way that he lived his life that I was expected to do better than he had, just as he had done better than his father. The day I graduated from high school was a big deal to him; I knew how important he and my mother, a high-school drop out, viewed education. The day I became the first college graduate in our extended family of over 100 people was a huge accomplishment for both of us. He too had earned a piece of that sheepskin by the sacrifices he had made in order for me to be able to graduate debt-free on our family's limited income.

My husband and I expected more of our daughters, just as our parents had expected more of us, and they will in turn expect more of their children. Some may call this the American dream; I call it the progress of life. The climb up the staircase symbolizes our desire to do more than those who have come before us.

At this point in my life, I am both the mother and the child in this poem. I am the wife, mother, and teacher on the higher stair, encouraging my husband, daughters, and students to keep striving for the next level. I am still climbing my very own staircase, which is littered with obstacles and challenges to be overcome at home, at work, and at the School of Library Science. But I am also like the child; I need the encouragement and support of family, friends and colleagues to keep going when those very same challenges seem overwhelming.

This poem motivates me to finish my master's and to move on the next challenge, National Board Certification. It reminds me to encourage others to keep striving to overcome the obstacles along their life's staircase—whether those are abuse, low self-esteem, poverty, racism, or limited English proficiency. We are on that staircase together and we all have to keep going regardless of whatever happens or gets in our way.

* * *

SCHEFT'S RESPONSE

There are several things that moved me about Carron's piece, but none more than her relationship to the poem's characters:

At this point in my life, I am both the mother and the child in this poem. I am the wife, mother, and teacher on the higher stair, encouraging my husband, daughters, and students to keep striving for the next level. I am still climbing my very own staircase, which is littered with obstacles and challenges to be overcome at home, at work, and at the School of Library Science. But I am also like the child; I need the encouragement and support of family, friends and colleagues to keep going when those very same challenges seem overwhelming.

Reading that paragraph was clearly an "aha! moment" for me. When we are first exposed to the poem, we are usually young (middle grades students), and we can only identify with the son. And that identification never ends. But, as Carron explains, as we go through the stages of life, as our roles expand, we connect with the poem similarly ... and differently.

*   *   *

Editor's Note: Melissa Davis is an academic coach at Green Acres Elementary School in Smyrna, GA. Melissa is the founder of 4 The Kids Learning Program (4KLP), which provides a free after-school service to 15 to 30 at-risk students. The 4KLP program includes homework assistance, spiritual guidance, nutritious meals, and team-building skills.

Her husband, Jon, and three children—Alexis, Meagan, and Jonathan—keep her extremely busy with basketball, football, track, gymnastics, JROTC, public speaking, and band, not to mention the day-to-day duties of maintaining a home. She volunteers in her personally funded after-school program, but also at her local church 2 days a week where she works with the multimedia department at World Changers Church International in College Park, GA. Her daughter Meagan gave her the code-name "Super Mom." Says Davis, "I'm either super mom or super nuts."

Melissa dedicates this piece to her mother, Annie Mae Ware. " There is no one in this world I admire more," she says. "Not only did she shape my life and mold me into the woman I have become today, but she is and was one of the most important driving forces of my life. I agonized tremendously over this piece and how others would perceive her and how she would be portrayed through this one moment in time, as I struggled to recall a 5-year-old's repressed memory. I simply say to the reader, open your mind to the unending love of a strong, wise, formidable, powerful Black Southern-bred mother."

*   *   *

I first read the poem "Mother to Son" by Langston Hughes in college. It was such a reflection of the plight of my parents and grandparents that I later taught it to my daughter to present for a language arts project, instead of the assigned recitation of "A Snowy Day" by Robert Frost.

"Mother to Son" is a perfect example of fortitude. Even though times may get hard, there is never the option of giving up. I witness the quitting attitude in my students everyday. With stagnate replies of "It's too hard," "I don't know," and "Can't you just tell me?"—they don't seem to want to work for much of anything. For instance, I will ask my students to read a paragraph and highlight the important information in the paragraph. Five minutes later, I'll read the passage, and then ask the students to tell me what they highlighted as important. All too often many of them will say, "Well I didn't know what to highlight, so I didn't highlight anything." Sad but true.

This poem signifies that things won't always be easy, but no matter what comes their way, with a little hard work, determination, and self-confidence some people will succeed.

Although I was born in the mid-1960s, the school I attended in Pontotoc, Mississippi was still segregated in the early 1970s. By the second half of my first grade year, the desegregation laws were being enforced, my school was dismantled, and we were placed in the White schools. No one ever told us what happened to all of the African American teachers we once had.

My family and I lived in a four-room house, with no bathroom and no running water until I was 6 years old. Yes, I took a bath in one of those metal washtubs. We heated the water, which we pumped from the well, on top of a fire log stove/heater. My dad was a truck driver and my mom began working in a factory after I started school. My grandparents were maids, and sharecroppers, and—before that—slaves.

I grew up knowing that life was full of uncertainties. But I also knew that I always had someone I could depend on, whom I could trust and confide in—my mother. Like most little girls I idealized my mother. She was a very beautiful, slender built woman, standing about 5-feet tall, with long, coal-black, wavy hair. Her skin tone was a rich, smooth, creamy ivory color that accented her high cheekbones and thin, slanted brown eyes, which always seemed to sparkle. Her teeth were white as pearls and when she smiled, it just seemed to melt all your heartaches away. She was what Blacks back then called a "yellow-boned woman" or "high yellow." That simply meant that she was fair-skinned. She worked hard and sacrificed her needs and desires in order to help my father provide for our family.

I remember one time my brother, who was constantly in trouble for one reason or another was teasing me saying, "You know you're adopted."

"No I'm not!" I shouted, in a snotty kind of way.

"Yes you are!" he said. "Somebody left you on our doorstep when you were a baby, and mama and daddy felt so sorry for you because you were so pitiful that they kept you."

"You're telling a story," I said. Back then a child could not say the word lie; instead they had to say "story" for made-up or an untruth.

"No I'm not!" he responded. "Can't you see you don't look like any of us?"

By the way I look much like my mother, but at that point I was running and yelling back at him, "I'm going to tell mama!" and off I went. I found my mother in the kitchen preparing our meal and I asked her, "Mama, am I adopted?"

She looked at me in a puzzled way and said, "Now where would you get an idea like that?" She paused slightly. "Never mind. JAMES!" she yelled. Then she said to me with a smile on her face, "If you were adopted, do you think you would still be living here? Now go out and play."

I don't know what she did to my brother that day, but it didn't matter.

My sisters, brother, and I, without ever hearing it, knew that she loved us unconditionally.

Not too long ago many of us were able to take for granted a mother's love, patience, and understanding spirit. These traits were automatic, almost a prerequisite for being a mom—but not any longer. Too many of our students don't experience this type of affection. Therefore, they look to us—their teachers—for more than just an education, but as mother/father, psychologist, doctor, and confidant.

Knowing that this tremendous gift to be a teacher has been given to me, I take every opportunity to persuade each child that they have a chance to make a difference. Thus, I start the school year by taking my students on a field trip to the Dr. Martin Luther King, Jr. Center in Atlanta, GA. While visiting the center, the students are usually in a state of disbelief as to what they see. They sit in the theater and observe in dismay as young children are sprayed with high-powered water hoses, and as rocks are hurled at them from an arm-length away—for no other reason than attempting to go to school with White children, as the police, who are supposed to protect and serve, set dogs loose to mangle and maim anyone of color in their path. It's hard for many of them to wrap their psyches around the possibility that those types of travesties could have ever happened. One time, as we sat in the King Theater, watching these events from the past become a part of our reality, one of my students leaned over and asked, "Mrs. Davis, can we leave now? I don't want to see anymore."

With tears streaming down her face and a few swelling up in my eyes as well, I said, "It's almost over now, but you don't have to watch any longer." And she closed her eyes tightly and laid her head on my shoulder.

Later at school, when discussing the trip, I explain portions of what I witnessed and experienced growing up in a rural area of Mississippi. How I had to be punished by my mother for hugging a White teacher. Please don't misunderstand. My mother is a warm, caring, and nurturing woman who loves her children more than life itself. It's not that she wanted to whip me, but it's what she felt she had to do in order to keep me from being punished by someone who didn't care about me. There are many scenarios for her reasoning during those changing times, such as the possibility of my being put out of school, being mistreated by the teacher later, teaching me my proper place while in a racist school setting, and perhaps by her disciplining me instead, keeping me from hating school and teachers later. Little did I know, the teacher whom I felt compelled to hug was a racist and extremely agitated at my blatant disregard for protocol. I did not truly realize the depth of my mother's love, the reason for my punishment, and the pain she must have suffered, until I was in college and read "The Ethics of Living Jim Crow, An Autobiographical Sketch" by Richard Wright. In this story a few young Black and White boys are throwing cinders across the tracks at each other. During the cinder war the White boys switched from cinders to broken glass. In the Black boys' retreat, Wright was hit behind the ear, opening a deep wound that bleed heavily. A neighbor took him to a doctor, who put three stitches in his neck. At night when his mother came from the White folks' kitchen, he raced down the street to meet her, to tell of his encounter with the White boys. He stated, "She grabbed a barrel stave, dragged me home, stripped me naked, and beat me till I had a fever of one hundred and two." In between the licks she told him "never, never, under any conditions, to fight *White* folks again. She finished by telling me that I ought to be thankful to God as long as I lived that they didn't kill me."

In my life lesson to my students, I remind them of the importance of an education and how it separates us from ignorance. I begin with a brief history of Mississippi and how at that time Blacks were just being allowed to attend the White schools. "I was entering first grade during the second semester of school," I say, "on perhaps my second or third day and I was so excited."

I explain that I was only 5-years-old and when I saw my teacher, I ran up to her and hugged her around the knees. That's all I could reach at the time. Before I knew it, I was in the principal's office with the teacher being spanked by my mother. Not a word was spoken to me and I had no idea what the punishment was for at that very moment. However, my older sister who had witnessed me hugging Mrs. Griswall—an older, grey-haired White lady—later asked me, "What did you think you were doing?"

I asked, "What ... what did I do?"

She said, "With Mrs. Griswall, what were you thinking?"

I told her, "All I did today was hug my teacher."

She said, "Mrs. Griswall is one of the biggest racists at this school."

I, of course, didn't know what the word "racists" meant, but I figured it wasn't something good.

As I share a few more personal occurrences, I usually witness a few tears here and there and sometimes I shed a few of my own. Yet, I ask my students not to shed tears, but rather to use their lives as a testament of how grateful and fortunate they are to be recipients of the hard work of so many sacrificing people.

There are many reasons why I teach today, but one of the main reasons that stays forever engraved in my heart is because of people like Dr. King, who paved a road of freedom and justice for all, and James Meredith, who was the first Black to integrate Ole Miss University in Mississippi, and for my parents and grandparents who made many sacrifices to send me to college. I choose to live my life as a tribute to those who stood for the rights of all people—for those who worked as slaves and as sharecroppers, to make a better future for their families; who walked on wood and dirt floors, cleaned houses, and took care of other people's babies; who worked in factories, sewers, and ditches just to make ends meet; and for those who didn't give up when life got hard. I too understand, just as they did, quitting is NOT an option.

* * *

SCHEFT'S RESPONSE

When Melissa read this in class, a number of students teared up. Several cried. It's not hard to wonder how you would have reacted, had you been in her shoes. That's something the three stories in this chapter share—the ability to persevere in the most demanding of situations. It's not always easy to ask yourself: WHAT MIGHT I HAVE DONE?

The scene that had the most impact on me was the spanking in the principal's office—that little 5-year-old snatched up from her jubilant encounter with her new teacher, finding herself in the midst of stone-faced adults, and then for no seeming reason, being whipped in front of everyone by the person she most loved and trusted. And while I knew WHY it happened, why it HAD to happen, I was aware that many of my students were absolutely bewildered—stunned and staggered like the little 5-year-old. But these were professional educators, men and women decades older than the little girl, unable to fathom what was going on, sucked into a whirlpool of extreme disequilibrium. You could see it on their faces. WHAT JUST HAPPENED? IS SHE MAKING THIS UP? IS THIS SOME KIND OF FICTION?

And I remembered learning how slave parents—perpetually terrorized that their children would be taken from them, sold away never to be seen again—would publicly rebuke, ridicule, and punish their children IN FRONT of their oppressors—what some might misguidedly, euphemistically call a "coping strategy." And while I am—literally—processing this in seconds during Melissa's reading, I am looking into the faces of many of my students, who—as talented and learned as they may be—have been plunged into a frightening world they had never been truly aware of, never dreamt of.

And while Melissa reads on, I see these particular listeners struggle—intellectually drowning, trying to grab on to something, anything … some sense of meaning, some kind of clarity. They sit there—calmly enough on the outside, but their minds flail—desperately seeking understanding. For some, it will come quickly. For others, this agony will continue. And finally, as Melissa ends her piece, while many sit there—eyes cast down, emotionally spent, hands shoot up from all parts of the room. And I know EXACTLY what their questions and comments will be … because I've been doing this teaching "thing" for a while. And I know—but not exactly—what I will need to do, what I will TRY to do to guide my students.

CHAPTER 9

IN THE BLOOD

Joshua Knight

Editor's Note: Joshua Knight currently works on a Multisystemic Treatment Team (MST), which allows him to work with adolescents. "Although it's referred to as a team, it doesn't quite conform to the traditional team format. We are a group of therapists utilizing the same treatment modality, and we share case information with each other on a weekly basis during group supervision, which allows us to learn from each other and provide feedback and different perspectives," he says.

"I work with children and their families to assist the children in overcoming social and behavioral challenges. This includes completing assessments, problem conceptualization, treatment planning, intervention implementation, continuous assessment of effectiveness in clinical treatment, and so forth," Josh explains. He works with children with severe anti-social behaviors, such as those diagnosed with conduct disorder or oppositional defiant disorder. MST is an intensive, home-based, short-term treatment (3-5 months) originally developed to be a cost-efficient, clinically effective treatment for juvenile offenders.

Prior to this Josh was a QMHP (Qualified Mental Health Professional) on an ACT (Assertive Community Treatment) Team, which provided intensive services for adults with mental illnesses like schizophrenia and bipolar disorder. He described it as being part of "a hospital without walls." While having worked in this role for about 2 years and finding it "very rewarding," Josh prefers working with children.

"When I'm not working, I'm doing school work," he notes. "I'm in my second year of a 3-year, part-time master's of social work program at UNC-Chapel Hill. It seems like they want to bury us in readings and I usually have

Inspiring Student Writers: Strategies and Examples for Teachers
pp. 87–92

a couple of projects going at any given moment. It's a great program though, and I'm learning a lot."

His favorite thing to do is "hang out with my girls"—his wife and daughter (age 4). "We go to the park, the pool, the mall, play with neighbors, fly kites, etc. We also go the gym together," he says. "If I had to pick a single hobby for myself, it'd be working out. I'll either jog at a nearby park before going to work in the morning or go to the gym during lunch if I can fit it in." Recently, Josh bought a red Doberman puppy, "a dog I've always dreamed of having." So now he splits his exercise time between going to the gym and taking Drake (the dog) for runs around the park or around the lake.

*   *   *

INTRODUCTION BY SCHEFT

Josh's piece begins in a familiar manner for lots of us, especially if you are a teacher: *I've always loved working with kids.* Many of us instantly identify with that line.

I certainly felt that way and have continued to feel that way for DECADES, although I never realized how fortunate I was. One day a few years ago, I was talking about career choices with a friend who is a psychologist. I believe I was being hard on a student (probably in his early twenties) who, according to me, was just floundering around, unsure of his future. I thought my friend, a pretty no-nonsense kind of therapist, would share my view. "When did you know what you wanted to do with your life?" he asked.

I thought for a moment. "I probably knew I wanted to be a teacher by the time I was ten. Definitely by the time I was eleven," I said.

We looked at each other for a few seconds. Then he spoke in a forceful, measured voice: "Do you have any idea how incredibly lucky you were?"

I didn't get his point. He must have seen that on my face, because he said again, "Do you have any idea how very lucky you were? It is rare for someone that young to have such a clear idea of their future. You were really lucky."

I started to get it. After a few minutes ... I got it.

Part of this life journey we take is all about trying to find our identity. For some of us, like me, it happens rather quickly. We avoid a lot of the dread and anxiety others face.

Teaching is a tough job, but like any line of work, if you know you're where you are supposed to be, then you are armed with a confidence that is invaluable—especially when confronted by the dilemmas inherent in any job.

I say all of this as a way of understanding the author of this piece. When he wrote this, he was a young man doing a job many of us could not do. And would not do. Some of us would turn it down in terms of being unprepared. But more of us would turn it down for lack of confidence in ourselves.

Actually, that's a nice way of saying we'd be too terrified.

* * *

IN THE BLOOD

I've always loved working with kids. I suppose it's in my blood. My mother worked with children for what seems like my entire childhood. I have so many memories of visiting her workplace as a child at the RSPCC (Rochester Society for the Prevention of Cruelty to Children). Although I don't remember it, my mother tells stories of me "taking up for" the "handicapped" students when my fellow elementary schoolmates would tease them. I'd walk with them to class as if I were their own defender of verbal abuse. So for one reason or another, I've always been partial to children from disadvantaged backgrounds. I've always believed that they need our help the most.

During my undergraduate college career, I read an amazing book by Edward Humes, *No Matter How Loud I Shout*. This book is a journalistic piece, detailing a failed juvenile justice system, while at the same time instilling hope for a brighter future in the reader. This book truly strengthened my desire to make a difference. One passage in particular moved me. The raw honesty and brutal reality of the passage touches something in me each time I read it.

> *These are the things I learned when I was growing up:*
> *I learned how to take a spray can of paint*
> *and write my nombre on the wall.*
> *I learned how to make a Walkman's motor into a tattoo machine,*
> *so that I could get my barrio on my arms and my neck,*
> *to show how much I love my homeboys.*
> *I learned how to sell the weed and the rock.*
> *These are the things I learned when I was growing up.*
>
> *When I was growing up, I learned how to take*
> *Another person's car without a key,*
> *how to drive it and sell it, or just leave it somewhere.*
> *I learned how to sit down low*
> *and look out the windows for the enemy,*
> *to see them before they saw me.*
> *And, finally, when I was growing up,*
> *I learned how to load bullets into a gun.*

I learned how to carry it and aim it,
and I learned how to shoot at the enemy,
to be there for my homeboys, no matter what.

These are the things I learned when I was growing up.
But this is what I want to know:
I want to know, who is going to teach me
how to pick out the right baby carriage for my little girl?
Who is going to teach me how to make up a bottle,
or to change a diaper, or to buy baby food?
Who is going to teach me how to be a father?
How to take care of my family?
How to live a life—a normal life?
These are the things I never learned growing up.
Who will teach me now?

This poem was written by a 16-year-old boy named Elijah, whose best friend died in his arms, whose uncles all went to jail, whose grandmother was murdered, and who (at the time of the book's publication) had a baby of eight months he had never held due to his incarceration. Elijah's life situation reminds me of an old saying: "There, but for the grace of God, go I." Although I'm not a religious person, this adage is very meaningful to me. Like Elijah's poem, it reminds me to reserve judgment. It reminds me that each and every person is looking out at the world through a different lens, forged of different experiences.

When I graduated from college, my first job was working for the Department of Juvenile Justice and Delinquency Prevention. I was working with some of the same sort of young men as Elijah, and I loved it! I really felt like I was making a difference, like I was one of those teachers Elijah was hoping for.

I recall having a particular connection with one child who I'll call Paul, a tall, 14-year-old Puerto Rican student with a soft voice and one of those subtle tempers. He was the type of person who you wouldn't know was upset until he was hitting you; it was always a surprise to see Paul angry and gesticulating wildly, because it seemingly came from nowhere. One of the first things I noticed about Paul is that he wanted to go further in life than he had, but he didn't know how to get started because he had never tried applying himself in an educational setting. Yet he was determined to stay off of the streets and avoid reentering the penal system. There were several times when he'd talk about the legitimate jobs he and his brother would get once they both got out of jail.

Paul had his thug side, but he also had a side that wanted to be more, and I showed him that I respected both sides. He appreciated this and over the course of the year, Paul really opened up and became one of the few students who would consistently engage in daily classroom activities.

Before teaching, I had worked with Paul (as well as many of the other students) as a counselor technician in the cottage on campus where he lived. When I changed positions and began working in a teaching capacity in the school, Paul was amazed by this transition. He told me once that he was proud of me for "moving up in the world." I think seeing me make what, to him, was an awesome change, helped him see that he could do the same thing. I'd help him study for his GED or show him how to improve the structure of a sentence, but more than that, I was a role model and a coach. Over the time we spent together, Paul learned how to identify an adverb, but he also learned that he was far more powerful than he previously believed.

While writing this story, I kept trying to recall one strong, vividly emotional exchange between Paul and me. I wanted something I could add to the story so that the reader would get a true sense of the change that took place, and the struggle it was to get through that change. But the truth is that dramatic, tearful scene never happened with us. It was more like a series of slow and deliberate steps that we took together, with Paul allowing me the pleasure of helping him find a new path.

Still, there were times of sadness. Paul definitely led a troubled life, and he shared much of it with me. But when he shared his story, there were no tears shed. Paul's pain was expressed instead as a badge of honor, as a symbol of his strength and fortitude. In my experience, C.A. Dillon is not the sort of place where the kids allow themselves to convey intimate emotions. At Dillon, the only tears shed are in anger or pain; and even then, it's during or after a physical confrontation. Dillon is a place where kids curse each other out in class on a regular basis. Where, among the students, the threat of violence is ceaseless and the ideal environment for learning is rarely part of the equation. It is in this setting that Paul went from a child who wouldn't be bothered with even attempting to complete his assignment, to a student who didn't mind being the last one taking his test. Under the circumstances, that was a very big achievement.

When I think back on my own adolescence, there are only a few teachers or life instructors who really stand out. Of all the many people who've taught and influenced me, there is only a handful that I consciously recognize to be the type of teachers Elijah was referring to. These are the teachers who, for some reason, connected with me and taught me lessons that go beyond the classroom. Yet in doing so, they made the classroom lesson that much more inviting and sincere. Hopefully, I offered at least a little of this experience to Paul. I may never know what happened to him; at the time that I left Dillon, he was scheduled to be released within a year. But wherever his life takes him, I trust that he'll continue down that path we started on together. Not just in the classroom, but in all aspects of his life. That long-lasting effect is a piece of what a good teacher imparts to his students, at least the ones he is able to reach. This is the type of teacher I am inspired to be—as a professional, as a parent, and as a role model for those who may come after me.

* * *

AFTERWORD BY THE AUTHOR

When I wrote this, I was planning on going into education. Things have changed. What has remained the same, though, is my desire to make a lasting impression. But perhaps the substance of that impression is different. These days, I don't much care if my clients remember me or not. What I want to do is to help them achieve their own values and goals, to live the lives they want to live. If I can help bring them to a place where they develop new skills to mange what used to be insurmountable challenges, that's the lasting impression I'm interested in. I want to empower my clients so that when I'm gone, whether they remember me or not, they have the tools, information, supports, skills, and confidence that will improve the quality of their lives.

* * *

SCHEFT'S RESPONSE

There is significance to this piece that isn't obvious. Typically, as I work with writers, as I push them to deal with incidents that will have an impact on their audience, they write about striking, moving incidents—offering dramatic examples of obvious change and even transformation. The most dramatic example is the one I mentioned in chapter 1—a son's remembering past events about his father, memories that radically altered his perception of his parent and himself.

And when I worked with Josh on this piece, I kept probing him. Take the ending, for example. After the first draft I said to Josh, "So what happened to Paul?" I waited for some spectacular epilogue.

Josh said, "I don't know."

As famed anchorman Walter Cronkite used to say: "And that's the way it is" ... especially in education. Most of us don't know what happens to most of our students. Most of them don't become famous, successful celebrities or discovers of the cure for the common cold. They don't keep in touch. And so while this piece might not have the "wow factor" of some others, when you stop and consider what Josh is writing about, there's plenty of wow.

Sometimes it's easy to spot the hero—that firefighter rescuing the baby from the burning building, the soldier carrying a fallen comrade out of harm's way. But other heroes may not be so obvious ... at first.

CHAPTER 10

THE BLACK TEACHER

Marshella Reid

Editor's Note: Marshella Reid, an educator at Y.E. Smith Elementary School in Durham, NC, teaches second grade integrated with counseling, parenting, and nursing. Marshella, at Y.E. Smith since 2003, comments, "It's only been 5 years, but sometimes it feels like 50. I love my job, but at times it can be exhausting and comes with a lot of hard work. You have to be able to adapt to change and be ready for the many challenges that come your way." She recently earned her master's in elementary education, graduating with honors from North Carolina Central University. She is also a member of Alpha Kappa Alpha Sorority, Inc.

When she is not teaching, her favorite thing to do is shop. She shops all over, spending "the big bucks" she makes from teaching. "I wish we did make big bucks with all the challenging work we do," she notes. The most exciting places she has shopped are Paris and Italy, although she admits this happens when she is "sound asleep in the middle of the night." Her nieces think that she is rich because she constantly buys them things, but Marshella is "big on bargain shopping and getting the most out of my hard earned money."

Marshella eventually wishes to pursue her doctorate in education. Right now she is content with molding and shaping her second graders into bright, productive citizens.

* * *

Inspiring Student Writers: Strategies and Examples for Teachers
pp. 93–100

INTRODUCTION BY SCHEFT

Here is a discussion/journal exercise I pose to my students: Describe yourself in three words. They often choose an occupation/role (teacher, mother, father, counselor), gender, personal qualities (caring, creative, bloodthirsty [kidding]), geographic region (Foist and foremost, I gotta say I'm a Noooo Yawkah. Wha? You got a problem wid dat?). There's religion. And there's race.

Race. A lot of people—A LOT of people—do NOT want to talk about race for a variety of reasons. It can lead to some uncomfortable conversations … or worse … much worse. Feelings run deep, and many folks would like to keep them there, buried, hidden—if only for the moment.

I'm not one of them. Over the years I've had a number of students come to me and say (usually after class): "Why did you bring THAT up?" (They weren't merely being quizzical. Translation: What the hell are you doing forcing us to talk about THAT!?)

I routinely deal with racial concerns in my classes, because I feel race is one of the most important educational, psychological, and sociological issues. Period. We SHOULD deal with it. We MUST deal with it. (And if you think you're not dealing with it by not dealing with it, guess again.) Many of my students want DESPERATELY to discuss it, explore it, wrestle with it. Oftentimes students thank me for using class as a forum to discuss controversial issues, including race.

"But why can't we work toward a colorblind society?" say many bright, caring people.

That's a wonderful notion. I just don't see it ever happening in my lifetime. And I know "colorblindness" is an insensitive notion to many bright, caring people. They don't want their race homogenized, minimized, or sanitized. Their race is an integral, tangible, visceral part of who they are. They WEAR their race—literally and figuratively. And the last thing they want is for you NOT to see it, NOT to deal with it.

* * *

THE BLACK TEACHER

When I graduated from college in 2002, my aunt—who is an elementary teacher—gave me a poem called "The Black Teacher." Though becoming a teacher had always been a passion for me, after reading the poem, it really inspired me to give my all to my students.

THE BLACK TEACHER

Being a Black teacher makes you different from all others,
You were born in one culture and educated in another.
You are a legend of time,
You have a heart of gold,
You have so much to give,
You know so much that hasn't been told.

Black teachers, teach our children
The advantages we have over all other races,
The beauty, the creativity, the variety of colors, and shapes of faces.
Make our children believe that they can compete with anyone,
Help them understand that there's a time and place for seriousness
And a time for having fun.

Black teachers, stand tall for there are eyes upon you each day,
And little black ears that quickly take in every word you say,
Love them, teach them, and with them always be true,
So many dream of the day they'll someday be like you.

Black teachers, you're the ones on which
Many black children depend to be,
Parent, nurse, teacher, and friend,
Your hug may well be the first he's had for days,
Give freely and always find something you can praise.

Black teachers, don't criticize the black child,
Because he hasn't learned to read.
Don't let your colleagues tell you that black children can't succeed.
Be an advocate for black children, if it means going an extra mile,
Your rewards will be many and you'll end each day with a smile.

Black teacher, the challenges of your lives are before you today,
   will you meet them, will you greet them,
   or will you have nothing to say?
Will you stand silently knowing that our children are getting a raw deal?
If we don't speak out for them, black teacher, who will?

Being a black teacher makes you special, you see,
For no other teacher or educator's job compares with your responsibility!!!

—Eleanor Coleman

During my teaching career, I have noticed that Black students face many challenges that students of other races do not usually experience. The poem asks the question, "Will you stand quietly knowing that our children are getting a raw deal?" I keep this in mind every day, because

Black students sometimes do get a raw deal and I do not want any of my students to be another negative statistic.

It angers me when I observe how other teachers talk to and treat our Black children. I once heard a White first grade teacher comparing her students to dogs. She had them sitting on the carpet and said, "What is wrong with you guys? Y'all don't know a thing. Every last one of you are as dumb as dogs."

I approached her after school, explained that I overheard her telling the kids that they were as dumb as dogs, and that I did not appreciate it at all. I said, "How would you feel if a teacher was to make that statement to one of your sons? You were out of control and disrespectful. If this is the way you feel about these kids, you are in the wrong profession."

Seeing how angry I was, she knew not to say much. With a blank look on her face, she looked up and said, "I didn't mean to offend anyone. I was having a bad day."

"I don't care what type of day you may have had," I said, "but you don't ever compare any students to dogs. And do not apologize because you meant what you said."

I walked out and slammed the door. The principal was enlightened about the situation. The teacher resigned at the end of the year. However, I suspect other teachers feel similarly about our Black children.

Several teachers walk through the halls frustrated because they do not understand Black children and often do not know how to handle them. Most of the frustrated teachers I see are Caucasian. One day after school a teacher came to me literally in tears and asked me how do I do it. I said, "Do what?"

She said, "How do you get your students to behave? I've tried everything and they just won't listen. I am fed up and I do not know what else to do."

I told her that classroom management has to start from day one. I gave her some suggestions to help with classroom management, but evidently they didn't work for her.

There was another teacher who let her class run wild. I asked her why she didn't try to get her class in order. "I have become immune to their behavior and the best thing for me to do is to ignore them. Otherwise I will have a headache at the end of the day from yelling," she said. "Oh, and there is no help for half of them because they do not care. I am just trying to make it till the end of the school year."

I consider myself as a gift to my students because they have someone who can relate to them and understand the hardships and struggles they face. Those students whom teachers refer to as "bad" and "hopeless" are the students I ask to be in my class because I know that I can make a difference in their lives.

While looking for a job, I got offers from several types of schools. I chose to work at a Title 1 school where the population was predominately Black because I knew that these students needed me. I have been at the same school since I started my career. Many of the students look up to me because I constantly demonstrate my true love to them.

Three weeks ago I received a letter and a teddy bear from a former student. The letter read, "Ms. Reid, you are the best teacher that I have ever had. I would not be where I am today if it wasn't for you. Thank you for all that you have done for me. Love, Tammy."

Two years ago Tammy was viewed as "awful," "disrespectful," and "angry" by the teachers she had before me. She was a skinny, little Black girl who was the fourth sibling of nine children. She and her siblings argued nearly everyday at school. Tammy seemed upset most of the time, constantly wearing a frown. Her hair was combed in a ponytail most of the time—which looked wild and messy by the end of the day. The clothes she wore were often too big. Shirts would fall off her shoulders and pants sagged off her bottom because she rarely wore a belt. Many times I wondered how she was able to breathe, since her nose stayed dirty (despite the season), and I had to remind her several times throughout the course of the day to wipe it. She did not like anyone to touch her and would curse out students frequently.

About three days into the school year, Tammy developed an attitude with me and stomped to her desk, saying, "That's why I can't stand this class!"

I laughed inwardly for a second—not a good laugh—and called her back to my desk. I told her privately, "I do not know what type of teachers you are used to dealing with, but you are in Ms. Reid's class, and I am not going to put up with your attitude. You are not going to start your year off being disrespectful. I observed you last year and saw how you acted."

I rubbed her back and said, "Guess what? I wanted you to be in my class because I know you need a teacher like me."

As tears started falling down her face, she put her head down and said that she was sorry. From that point on, things were different between us. She wanted hugs everyday and those frowns began to turn into smiles. Though her attitude toward other people did not change over night, she respected me. We worked on her attitude throughout the year, and she gradually got better. Now she is a totally different child.

Experiences such as these keep me motivated to reach every child. I am an advocate for every child of all races, but no matter what, I am The Black Teacher.

* * *

SCHEFT'S RESPONSE

In the first chapter, I talked about the importance of dialogue. What we SAY is often linked to ACTIONS, which may provide crucial information for the reader. The encounter between Marshella and Tammy on the third day of the new school year is rendered vividly through the dialogue. First, we hear Tammy: *"That's why I can't stand this class!"* Then the teacher: *"I do not know what type of teachers you are used to dealing with, but you are in Ms. Reid's class, and I am not going to put up with your attitude. You are not going to start your year off being disrespectful. I observed you last year and saw how you acted."*

Okay ... that scene gets played out in hundreds of classrooms year after year after year. We can see the teacher's face; we can hear the abrupt, no-nonsense, even chilling tone. (For some of us, this conjures up an all too graphic memory.) And I remember how, as I continued reading Marshella's paper, the next four words STUNNED me:

I rubbed her back ...

Hey, I wasn't expecting that. Those four, simple words make such a powerful statement about Marshella, which is then augmented by the dialogue and the unmistakable change in tone: *"Guess what? I wanted you to be in my class because I know you need a teacher like me."*

Four little words, followed by 19 more—enough to take a tough, sad kid like Tammy and make her cry. Not tears of fear. Not tears of anger. Tears of epiphany. Tears of hope ... and promise ... and change.

That is the power of dialogue and action. We see and feel because we have been shown, not told.

*   *   *

I want to tell you a little bit about Eleanor Coleman, the author of "The Black Teacher," who graciously gave me permission to use her poem in my book. Ms. Coleman has been in education for over 35 years and currently serves as a counselor in the Little Rock School District of Arkansas. She is "very active" in the Little Rock Counselors and Teachers Association, the Arkansas Education Association, and the National Education Association (having served on the NEA Board).

She wrote "The Black Teacher" when she was president of the NEA Black Caucus. "I consider myself an inspirational writer," she told me. "I can only write about those things that I feel strongly about."

Some readers may be bothered by Ms. Coleman's poem, about a teacher seeing himself or herself as a "Black teacher." *ISN'T THAT A PROBLEM?*

they wonder. *WHAT IF SOMEONE CALLED HERSELF A "WHITE TEACHER"?*

I've heard this argument before. While it seems to proceed logically enough, it's based on the notion that Black and White experiences should somehow be the same, interchangeable. They are not.

To understand Ms. Coleman's poem, it helps to go back and look at the last sentence in Marshella's piece: *I am an advocate for every child of all races, but no matter what, I am The Black Teacher.* I have known a number of fine educators who would describe themselves, first and foremost, as Black teachers. Like Marshella, they serve all their students, but they would add that they have a special mission for some of their Black students, a mission Ms. Coleman refers to in her poem.

Similarly, I know other teachers who serve all their students, but they place a special emphasis on their female students, or their poor students, or their exceptional students, or some other group or race they feel needs an added little boost, an extra hand, another pat on the back. This falls under the realm of what the textbooks call "compensatory education." This concept is not about notions of superiority and inferiority. It is about compensation at no one's expense. To use a common expression, we're "leveling the playing field." Some of our students don't require a lot from us. Some. But others, as Ms. Coleman notes, need us to go "an extra mile."

I don't expect everyone to agree with me. I don't expect everyone to understand. Hey, it took me a while. Right now, I THINK I get it. I was brought up in an affluent, White world, and I didn't really consider the implications of being White (or NOT being White) until I was in my mid-twenties. My parents taught me not to be prejudicial toward anyone's race or religion, and I had no trouble accepting that and living by that code. However, years later when I heard the term "White male privilege," I became immediately upset. That term hit me hard. I was angry, resentful, defensive. I couldn't get past that label. IF YOU'RE TRYING TO MAKE ME FEEL GUILTY, I thought, YOU PICKED THE WRONG HONKY.

I calmed down. I needed to get over MY pre-judging. And when I did, when I explored the concept, I came—quite calmly—to a simple conclusion: Throughout my life I have benefited from being White, from being male. Sometimes it's been subtle. Sometimes it's been enormous.

I've never been hassled by the police. But most of my Black male students (old and young) have at least one powerful, disturbing story on this subject.

Except for my teenage years, I've never been followed when trying on clothes or shopping in a store. But many of my Black students (old and young) have had and continue to have this experience.

I have seen people ignore and even interrupt my female colleagues in order to get my opinion.

I understand my White male privilege. I try not to abuse it. But it's more than just my being White and male. I also have the distinct privilege of having wonderful parents who gave me constant love, guidance, and opportunities. I have been very fortunate and incredibly lucky. I still don't feel guilty. I feel grateful.

I am reminded of a friend, Cathy, who passed away a number of years ago. She was a reporter for a local TV station. She came frequently to the journalism classes at NCCU to talk to the students. She often began her discussions by saying, "You all know Ed Bradley, the famous reporter for 60 Minutes. He frequently tells people he is a journalist who happens to be Black. I, on the other hand, am a Black journalist. If the assignment doesn't involve the Black community, I'm not interested."

We don't all like the same stuff. That's why Baskin-Robbins creates a whole bunch of flavors.

The truth is we don't like all our students the same, just as we don't like all our friends the same. Often there is a best friend, some good friends, and those who may not make the next cut. And because we won't like all our students the same, we need to love them all. For some, this means giving them room, watching from afar. For others, it means reaching out, inserting ourselves in their lives (in and sometimes outside of school)—"going an extra mile."

While this may—sometimes—have to do with race, it may have absolutely nothing to do with race.

CHAPTER 11

DEALING WITH LIFE

Sloane Akos

Editor's Note: Sloane Akos is the media coordinator (a.k.a. "The Library Lady") at Triangle Day School, a small, private, K-8 school in Durham, NC. Before becoming "a licensed book pusher" to young children, she worked in a variety of student services jobs assisting college students at an assortment of Southern universities.

While she enjoys turning kids on to books, she most loves attempting, with her professor-counselor husband, to raise two self-reliant girls. When not gulping down the latest YA (young adult) and children's books, she strives to be a relatively late-bloomer, wannabe athlete, and semiprofessional iPod Nano user.

* * *

INTRODUCTION BY SCHEFT

North Carolina has a wonderful state motto: *esse quam videri* (to be rather than to seem). These words are about determining what is true and real and honest. While there is—indeed—a negative side to this, exposing that which is false and illusory and dishonest, the words are typically spun in a positive way. Teachers and parents often use the phrase for motivation, presenting us with the quest to be—at the very least—good. Beyond that is the implication of excelling.

Inspiring Student Writers: Strategies and Examples for Teachers
pp. 101–105
Copyright © 2009 by Information Age Publishing

As I write this, a lyric from one of my favorite writers, a guitar-smashing Brit by the name of Pete Townshend, pops up in my mind: Who are you?

Hmmm. Good question.

* * *

DEALING WITH LIFE

For the majority of my life, I always felt a little envious of people who always knew what they wanted—who they wanted to be, what they wanted to get, how they were going to achieve their goals. I'm speaking of those people who have such a passion you feel the fervor of their words when they speak. So driven are they it seems they simply journey straight through life to their purpose. I'm a dabbler—a little of this and a little of that. I'm interested in a lot of things, being good at a few, and intrigued enough with others to keep learning. That overriding sense of certain purpose has always eluded me.

Then I took those first, self-reflecting counseling courses while working towards my initial graduate degree, and I came across so many people who had experienced such tribulations. No one was untouched. Their individual misfortunes had pushed them; they had faced adversity and found insight. I often felt, honestly, guilt for the lack of misfortune in my life. I had surely experienced the regular ups and downs of adolescence and families in general, but no real "At That Moment" event. I was floating along on the wave of my life, just enjoying the ride and where it took me.

Why was I unaffected? Surely, I should be doing something "BIG" with my life. After all, I had lived with virtually no impediments. Often, I felt tremendous self-reproach; I hadn't paid homage to blessings I'd been given. I heard the stories of trauma, terror, and loss, and I wondered when the other shoe was going to drop. When would the time come where I would have to step up and see if I had the grit to determine my providence?

For my family, that other shoe dropped August 7, 2002, when a military C-130 crashed in Puerto Rico. Everyone on board was killed, including my 33-year-old brother-in-law, the pilot. The Akos boys' middle brother was gone, his wife without a husband, his parents now without their son, Mike. My husband and I were 7 months pregnant with our second child and yet, for a long while, the possibilities and opportunities of life stood still.

In our collective grief, we often marveled—and still do—at how big a life Mike led. He would try anything at any given time—swim with sharks at Alcatraz, trek the backwoods of North Carolina, jump out of planes, and—my favorite—place in a race after an all-night party. He is remembered for his humor, his humility, and his generosity. He was affably tenacious.

Mike was an Air Force Special Operations pilot, part of the covert operations no one really admits to or even discusses. It might even make you uncomfortable to think about. You're picturing buzz-cut, Top Gun, rigid professional; Mike was the antithesis of this stereotype. He was anything but covert and uncomfortable.

His manner was open and welcoming. He was your next-door neighbor, complete with ragged golf visor and well-worn flip-flops—a grown-up version of that mischievous little boy down the block, reveling in practical jokes and slapstick humor. Mike had these novelty plastic teeth—not the Dracula fangs—the country, brown, rotted out, never-seen-a-toothbrush kind he loved. As long as I knew him, you could be carrying on a conversation with him, and suddenly, those nasty teeth would be peeking out from his crooked smile. Everyone around is cracking up like kids in the back of the classroom and Mike is looking around saying innocently, "What?" Envision a brown haired version of *Dennis the Menace* or *Calvin* with a great supply of Cuban cigars.

My point: Mike's life was not a practice run; it was his full life, every day. He did not wait to see what life would make of him. He was who he wanted to be.

Mike's burial at Arlington National Cemetery was held September 4, 2002.

In retrospect, I marvel at how fast and how loud that other shoe can be when it falls. That deafening thump reverberates. Sometimes I wake up in the middle of the night and lie very still, listening to the night noises, my husband's snores, and my daughters' dream-filled mutterings. I replay my life and think, *Have I missed something?* Then I think about who I've become and what I've yet to do. I fall back to sleep, in comfort, thinking of the things I want to try next.

Tragedies happen every day. Life is lost all the time. My story is not so different. Certainly, heartbreak is not a mandatory element. I know this now. Passion is not a place; *passion is what you determine it to be.* At any given moment, I can decide what I'm going to do; the only contingents being my own consideration, consistency, and the number of days I've been given. I recognize this is all the reverence I ever need convey, not only to my God, but also to my family and myself.

I know life is a timorous opportunity. My road will always be rambling and wide versus straight and narrow. This is my chosen path; it's what keeps me interested and motivated.

Every day, I have the choice to be a critic or a supporter.

I choose either to yell and blame, cry or whisper, praise and laugh.

I can be an enabler or a motivator.

I can dig deeper or I can simply give up.

I am, at this very moment, an athlete, a student, a daughter, a sister, a mother, a lover, a friend.

Whatever I choose this day, I can be.

And every day, I am a grateful believer.

We are what we repeatedly do.

—Aristotle

*   *   *

AFTERWORD BY THE AUTHOR

I still don't know exactly why I felt I needed to write about our loss. Perhaps it was because I felt so disconnected to my then still relatively new family. I was an outsider in a huge family affair and I didn't know if, when, or how to help. My husband and I struggled privately and, mostly, separately. He felt he needed to keep everyone moving and keep some semblance of normalcy for us. I was overwhelmed being so pregnant and having to chase a toddler. The surrealism seemed to stretch so long because of investigations, getting everyone home, and all the memorials.

Grief affects us all so differently; in reflection, this piece is, finally, my personal, public eulogy of my brother-in-law. We call our youngest daughter after him—Riley Mike.

AKOS, MICHAEL J.
MAJ US AIR FORCE
VETERAN SERVICE DATES: 07/03/1992 - 08/07/2002
DATE OF BIRTH: 05/06/1969
DATE OF DEATH: 08/07/2002
DATE OF INTERMENT: 09/04/2002
BURIED AT: SECTION 66 SITE 7134
ARLINGTON NATIONAL CEMETERY

*   *   *

SCHEFT'S RESPONSE

When students write about the death of someone to whom they've been close, the first drafts—typically—don't convey much about the person. It's understandable. The writer—so immersed in emotion, so overwhelmed by the task—usually feels a need to express (over and over) how important, how good, how inspiring their person was. There is a lot of telling, but not much showing. This is normal.

When I point this out to students, they understand, and I then convince them of the need for revision that incorporates some physical description and some memorable illustrations that might include dialogue. "Remember," I tell them, "the readers don't know this person. You've got to introduce them to us. We need to SEE them. We need illustrations, stories, examples that help us understand WHY they were so meaningful, so influential."

Sloane does an excellent job of capturing Mike for us. We see him. We hear him. We get him.

Sloane's piece also speaks to another aspect of this assignment. One purpose of this paper is to feed the soul of the author. Beyond that, however, is the audience. This becomes our paper too. Through the ending of the paper and the Aristotle quotation, Sloane explains her transformation. If you think it's merely reportorial, dear reader, you miss the point.

Look in front of you. Right in front of you. There … on the ground. I believe that's a gauntlet.

Esse quam videri, y'all.

CHAPTER 12

A RENEWED SENSE OF LIFE

Jayne Dorfman

Editor's Note: Jayne Dorfman has been a children's librarian for over 14 years. She loves the art of storytelling and has always specialized in Children's Services. She began her career in public librarianship but after several years this was "just not chaotic enough," and she moved into the school system. Ms. Dorfman is the school librarian at an urban elementary school with over 750 students. She loves the challenge of getting her students hooked on books. Most of her students do not have a "print rich" environment at home. Ms. Dorfman's mantra is "I never, EVER, met a child who did not love a good story!"

Ms. Dorfman has raised one reader of her own, daughter Isabella, age 8, and is working on Catalina, age 5. For the most part, she spends her free time contemplating her personal role in closing the achievement gap. She also jogs to relieve stress, trains young horses, and—of course—loves a good book.

* * *

SCHEFT INTRODUCTION

This piece starts out with an interesting device. Even though the work is nonfiction, the writer creates a fictional character and presents him to the reader—briefly—at a particular time and place. Although there aren't

Inspiring Student Writers: Strategies and Examples for Teachers
pp. 107–112
Copyright © 2009 by Information Age Publishing

many details, the reader tends to connect with the character—perhaps in terms of his vulnerability, his sense of doubt.

As I discuss throughout this book, it is often hard for us to admit our shortcomings—unless someone else admits theirs first. After the ice is broken, we gain courage—knowing we are not alone. Establishing this connection so immediately is an effective way of "hooking" the reader and is a clear strength of this chapter.

*   *   *

A RENEWED SENSE OF LIFE

The sound of the bell rang out through the dark hallways. The novice monk woke slowly from a deep sleep. He had been here in the monastery for nearly 6 months and still could not get used to the 3:00 A.M. gathering for prayer. It was dark. It was cold. He had only been asleep for 3 hours since the last prayer cycle at midnight and he knew he would be up and at it again at 6:00 A.M. He wondered if all this prayer was really necessary. He heard his brothers stirring and reluctantly rose from the warm bunk. A few minutes later he entered the candlelit chapel and added his voice to those of his brothers. As always, the beauty of the words and the message filled him with a different kind of warmth. Alone, perhaps his voice could not make a difference. But added to that of others, a stronger voice was created that just maybe could change things for the better.

> In the tender compassion of our God,
> the dawn from on high shall break upon us,
> to shine on those who dwell in darkness
> and the shadow of death,
> and to guide our feet on the road of peace.
> Glory be ...

That passage is from the scriptures, the *Benedictus*, a part of the morning prayers of the traditional daily prayer cycle that comes from Catholic monastic life. The prayers are said throughout the day for guidance and inspiration. In monasteries, this also includes prayer at midnight and 3:00 A.M. Monks are literally praying for the world around the clock.

For many years, I struggled with identity and purpose. I was labeled as academically gifted. Because of a troubled family life, I clung to this as a source of self-esteem and overidentified with it. What were my talents and how should I use them? What was my role in the world? Because of these struggles, I was ineffective and underdeveloped as a person. Professionally, personally and interpersonally, I was not fulfilled and felt like I was failing to live up to expectations. I came to realize that it was uncomfortable for others when I kept changing my path and plan. However, this is not something I could change easily or solve quickly. But my awareness was a beginning.

Over time, I began to find direction. This was based on a growing sense that relationships are the most important things in my world. The death of a brother, the birth of my first daughter, and the collapse of a personal dream led to this realization. People are truly more important than things.

The call about my brother's death shocked me into a state of personal upheaval. Freddy had committed suicide at the age of 41. Our family had failed to save him. Many years of dysfunction had left my family fractured and distant from one another. And now, we had a very painful and tragic situation to come through together. My brother had been unwilling to accept therapy or medication for his severe depression and finally made the decision to end his life. When he died, our family was challenged far beyond anything we had experienced before.

For a while, things hung in the balance. Were we going to choose life, to try to connect to each other and create a new family dynamic based on communication and truth? Or would this drive us even deeper into group denial and repression? Not long after Freddy's death, I chose life. I chose to love, to feel pain, and to try to build a new family. Fortunately, I was not the only one in my family who made this choice.

My renewed sense of life had other benefits. Exactly one year after my brother's death, December 9th, my first child was born. She was the first grandchild in our family, a living symbol of the changes and commitments we were celebrating together.

As I held my baby and fed her at my breast, I felt needed in ways that I had never experienced before. It was scary. I realized I would never be an individual in the same way again. I had a tremendous responsibility that would never truly end. It is an understatement to say that my view of my life completely changed. Plans and dreams I lived for crumbled when Isabella entered the picture.

The transformation to parenthood was physical as well. Before, I was a slender young woman who took joy in making her 2,000-pound equine partner move like a dancer and brought home so many blue ribbons that I used them to decorate the house. I fought to keep that as long as I could, but the arrival of my second daughter, Catalina, was the beginning of the end. Fifteen pounds heavier, tired, and stressed, I sold my horse, Tango, and gave myself up to my family, my career and my community.

There is always a lot of pain involved in personal growth, but I also began to feel a peace I had never felt before. As I began to commit to my family and community, I had the sense of calm and happiness that comes from a good decision. I was working on being in a right relationship with those around me, from my husband to the service person at the store. Thank you, Freddy and my girls, for giving me the courage to make big changes that I would never have made on my own.

I strive to make communication and understanding the goals of conflict interactions. It is difficult to express clearly my wants while respecting and working toward the wants of others. A solution that honors all parties leaves the doors of opportunity and partnership open.

I have a clearer idea of what I want my role in the world to be and how to best offer my skills. Teaching, especially through books, is a good way for me. I have more confidence in my skills and talents and how to put them to best use. I seldom doubt how I am spending the precious time I have here in this reality. The book is not yet closed on my personal dream. As I begin to settle into my career and as my children grow up, I see myself having time and energy again to find that young woman who still loves to work with horses.

Tears came to my eyes when I first read the scripture passage. I read it frequently as a celebration of life and the potential miracle of human and divine love. It never fails to set my feet firmly on my path to peace, within and without, when I begin to lose my way.

* * *

AFTERWORD BY THE AUTHOR

Books have always been a big part of my life. As a young person, I turned to books to find escape and peace. It was my way to live in a world that was orderly but exciting. In books I was faced with big problems, but they always had a satisfying resolution.

That is probably why I am a children's librarian. I deeply appreciate the power of books, especially in the life of a young person.

When I wrote this piece, I did not know it, but I was taking a big step. For most of my life I was a reader, then a book expert. With this piece, something interesting happened. I saw the power of my own stories. In short, I began to think and act like a writer.

I am currently working on a chapter book for middle grade readers. The themes are similar to those in my reflection piece: despair, courage and rebirth. My relationship with books is better and stronger than ever. Of course, I am still a big reader. I am still a book expert and love matching young people with just the right book. But now, I may even be a writer, giving life to my own stories. And someday, that "just right book" that I put in a child's hands ... might be my own!

*   *   *

SCHEFT'S RESPONSE

When people write so openly about themselves, it is hard for the reader NOT to self-reflect. These kinds of pieces have a Rorschach-test quality to them. (Remember the doctor who showed ink blot designs to his patients to get them to reveal their underlying personality?) Chances are no two people will react to this paper in exactly the same way. It's also amazing which sentences, which images connect with readers.

Toward the end of the chapter, Jayne writes:

> I have a clearer idea of what I want my role in the world to be and how to best offer my skills. Teaching, especially through books, is a good way for me. I have more confidence in my skills and talents and how to put them to best use. I seldom doubt how I am spending the precious time I have here in this reality. The book is not yet closed on my personal dream. As I begin to settle into my career and as my children grow up, I see myself having time and energy again to find that young woman who still loves to work with horses.

Dreams. That's an interesting place to visit. After student teaching, I began my "real" teaching career. First assignment: seventh graders. Okay, I had the job. Now what? Day one—what was I going to do?

I've always been a fan of thematic units, and after racking my brain and discussing things with my favorite teacher, Dr. Sterling Hennis, we came up with myths and fables. As I started to expand upon that general idea, I figured it might work if I started with dreams. Sure. Everyone has dreams.

But then I stopped. Dreams were so personal, often embarrassing. Would seventh graders be open to that? No, I reasoned, they wouldn't. And so I planned to introduce the concept, see if anyone volunteered (knowing full well these self-conscious teens wouldn't), and then branch off—rather briskly—into the dream-like world of mythology.

Day one of the school year, 1971. I had three classes—each a 2-hour block. First class. After a brief bit of background on myself (maybe two minutes), I switched gears. "I want to talk about dreams. Scientists say that while we may not remember them, we all have four or five dreams a night. Does anybody want to share one of your dreams?"

Every hand went up.

We shared our dreams for the first hour. Then the bell rang. Groans filled the room. "That's just the bell signaling the end of the first hour," I said. "We still have an hour left."

Cheers.

We needed most of that next hour to finish hearing from everybody. And it was a similar response in the other two classes.

My point: We are hungry to discuss our dreams. Oh we may be reluctant or deeply embarrassed, but our dreams are often at the core of who we are ... or—perhaps—who we WANT to be.

Langston Hughes explains it so poignantly. Life without dreams, says the poet, is empty, bleak, painful, unfulfilled, tragic—"a broken-winged bird that cannot fly," "a barren field frozen with snow." Decades later a rock and roll song would paraphrase Hughes' plea: Hold on tight to your dreams.

Indeed, hold on.

CHAPTER 13

THE POWER OF IMAGINATION

Taheera Blount

Editor's Note: Taheera Blount is a recent graduate of North Carolina Central University's Counselor Education Program. She is a member of several professional organizations—The American Counseling Association, The American School Counseling Association, The North Carolina Counseling Association, and The North Carolina School Counselor Association. She is an active member of her counseling honor society, Chi Sigma Iota.

Taheera obtained her bachelor of social work from Barton College in 2004. She worked 2 years as a clinical case manager with at-risk youth and their families before making the transition to graduate school. "I enjoyed my work, but it was extremely stressful," she said. "I had a huge case load. I didn't feel I was having the impact I wanted or needed to have."

During her spare time, Taheera enjoys spending time with family, reading ("mostly motivational books"), and scrapbooking. Scrapbooking? "I do the usual pasting of pictures and create designs around them," she said, "but I also create pages that focus on my goals and dreams." For example, when she wanted to be a graduate assistant, she created a card on her wall that spelled out her dream and she augmented it with sayings: "I will have this assistantship." "I will be a capable graduate assistant." "Believe." Less than a month later, she had the job. "My dreams come true for me," she declared.

* * *

Inspiring Student Writers: Strategies and Examples for Teachers
pp. 113–121

INTRODUCTION BY SCHEFT

I don't like to stereotype or generalize, but—unfortunately—I'm a human being, so I tend to do this every now and then. Before Taheera was my student, I saw her at least once a day in the School of Education—a polite, smiling, energetic graduate assistant … one of those "smilers" who just make you feel good. This was—and continues to be—part of a very comfortable "vibe" she radiates.

I didn't know anything about her, except that all those who worked with her loved her dependable, "can do" spirit. I sized her up as someone who had probably lived a pretty comfortable, stress-free life … popular … perhaps a cheerleader in high school … maybe from a wealthy family … a product of the good life.

Yup. That's what I thought.

*   *   *

THE POWER OF IMAGINATION

YESTERDAY, I CRIED
By Iyanla Vanzant

> *Yesterday, I cried.*
> *I came home, went straight to my room, sat on the edge of my bed,*
>   *kicked off my shoes, unhooked my bra,*
>   *and I had myself a good cry.*
> *I'm telling you,*
>   *I cried until my nose was running all over the silk blouse I*
>   *got on sale.*
>   *I cried until my ears were hot.*
>   *I cried until my head was hurting so bad*
>   *that I could hardly see the pile of soiled tissues lying on*
>   *the floor at my feet.*
> *I want you to understand,*
>   *I had myself a really good cry yesterday.*
> *Yesterday, I cried,*
>   *for all the days that I was too busy, or too tired, or too mad*
>   *to cry.*
> *I cried for all the days, and all the ways,*
>   *and all the times I had dishonored, disrespected, and discon-*
>   *nected my Self from myself,*
>   *only to have it reflected back to me in the ways others*
>   *did to me*
>   *the same things I had already done to myself.*
> *I cried for all the things I had given, only to have them stolen;*
>   *for all the things I had asked for that had yet to show up;*

for all the things I had accomplished, only to give them
    away, to people in circumstances,
which left me feeling empty, and battered and plain
    old used.
I cried because there really does come a time when the only thing left
    for you to do is cry.
Yesterday I cried.
I cried because little boys get left by their daddies;
    and little girls get forgotten by their mommies;
    and daddies don't know what to do, so they leave;
    and mommies get left, so they get mad.
I cried because I had a little boy, and because I was little girl, and
    because I was a mommy who didn't know what to do, and
    because I wanted my daddy to be there for me so badly until
        I ached.
Yesterday I cried.
I cried because I hurt. I cried because I was hurt.
I cried because hurt has no place to go
    except deeper into the pain that caused it in the first place,
    and when it gets there, the hurt wakes you up.
I cried because it was too late. I cried because it was time.
I cried because my soul knew that I didn't know
    that my soul knew everything I needed to know.
I cried a soulful cry yesterday, and it felt so good.
It felt so very, very bad.
In the midst of my crying, I felt my freedom coming,
Because
Yesterday I cried
    with an agenda.

Iyanla Vanzant uses her experiences to show how life's hardships can be re-languaged and re-visioned. These obstacles become lessons that teach us how to triumph over the challenges life brings us.

In the midst of those hardships and obstacles, we must know how to have a good cry. Growing up, I was often called a cry baby and even today at the age of 27, I have an occasional good cry. WHY DO I CRY SO EAS-ILY? I thought, as I read this poem. It was not until I read this poem that I found the meaning for my cry.

I am by nature an introvert. Growing up was not easy for me. At five years of age, I was known at school as "the dressing-up girl." A typical day for me included four ponytails each with ribbons to match my outfit, small gold hoop earrings, a colorful dress with white lace, black patent leather shoes from Stride Ride, white lace socks, and a sweater. My peers wore jeans and sneakers, but everyday my mother would make me dress up like a little girl. I often felt out of place. Even at the age of 5, one could witness the fear that shone on my face.

My mother was a 31-year-old medical office assistant, approximately 125 pounds, small in statue with a shaggy dog hairstyle. You might typically see her dressed in a black mohair turtleneck, brown wool blazer, and Jones New York black dress pants with a pair of high heel Nine West boots. She would often wear 14-carat gold hoop earrings and gold West Indian bangles. My mother was known in our apartment complex as a woman who "kept her appearance together." My father sold clothes, and he loved to outfit my mother. Both my dad and mom were involved in fashion; consequently, my mother established a large wardrobe. She was a woman of class.

On December 31, 1984, my mother received a telephone call from Bronx Lebanon Hospital stating that my father had passed away. For the first time in my life I witnessed my mother hollering and screaming. "I can't believe he is gone!" she wailed over and over. Suddenly, the classy woman who kept the family together began to shut down completely. My mother went into a state of depression—spending all day in bed, taking unnecessary days off from work. She found my father's death unmanageable. Because my mother could not cope, she began to find other ways to deal with the loss, which led to a lifestyle of addiction.

It was very difficult for me seeing my mother, a full-time worker and functional parent involved in her children's learning, deteriorate into an 85-pound, nonfunctional parent who didn't care about her appearance and family. During this time, I became even more withdrawn at school. It was very difficult for me to develop friends because of the turmoil I was experiencing at home. I always felt my life was different from my peers. At the playground, I would isolate and play by myself. The other children appeared to be happy, joyful, and enthused. I always had a sad and fearful expression upon my face. I never wanted to play with my peers. At the time I did not know the reason for this: I was worried about my mother and where this new life was going to take me.

On a winter day in 1985, my mother informed my siblings and me that we would have to stay with my grandmother. I cried and began to throw my toys because I was angry. I held on to my mother's leg and begged, "MOMMIE, DO NOT LEAVE ME."

She said that she had to get her life together. My mother promised that we would be safer with grandma and the option was either to stay with grandma or go into foster care with Social Services. My grandmother assured us that it would be in our best interest to stay with her. I worried that my mother would never come back to rescue me. I was very angry with my mother for leaving me. I would constantly wonder where my mother stayed during this period of my life. Since New York City is big, I would often look for my mother in the streets, especially from my bus seat as I commuted to and from school. I never saw her. Everyday, I wondered, WHEN IS MY MOTHER COMING BACK TO TAKE CARE OF US?

My mother became an absent parent for 1 year. Even though the decision to leave my mother was difficult, my grandmother's home turned out to be a loving, stable, and structured environment. Finally, since my father's death, I felt safe. I wanted to stay with my grandmother forever. I feared my mother would return with her drama. However, with my mother's arrival from detox treatment, she appeared to be a changed individual. She gained her weight back. Her clothes were intact and she seemed to care about us. "Kids, pack your belongings," she told us. "We are going to move to Harlem with my boyfriend, Toots."

WHO IS THIS TOOTS? I wondered. WHAT IS THIS GOING TO BE LIKE? I was scared because I had to meet new friends and live in a new area away from family. I was nervous, frightened, and disappointed that my mother would take me and my siblings to an unknown environment. I cried and cried because I had to leave my comfort zone and move with someone I did not know, my mother's boyfriend. But soon I moved with my brothers—Saledin, 11, and Faheem, 9. I knew they would protect me.

When we first met Toots, he appeared to be nice. He was approximately 185 pounds, 5'7", medium brown complexion with bifocal glasses. His normal clothing included a short-sleeve, checkered Oxford shirt with a pair of khakis. He had one leg, and he stayed mostly in a wheelchair, although when he went out with my mother, he'd put on a prosthetic leg.

I worried about when they went out. I wondered if my mother might start drinking again. And there was something about his presence that scared me. My mother reassured me that he was the best boyfriend she had met since my father's death. However, I knew deep down that this man had an ugly side.

It took about 2 weeks for it to emerge. Mornings began with Toots yelling, "KIDS, GET THE HELL UP! I MADE BREAKFAST FOR YOU!"

I began to pick up clues that my mother might be drinking again. And soon, it became clear she was. After a while, she would not get up in the morning. Most of the time, she would be asleep from the extensive hangover from the previous night. It became harder and harder for me to even see her.

When I wanted to talk with my mother, before I would enter his bedroom, Toots always discouraged me. He did not know how to talk to me in the proper tone. He was typically stern and hateful, controlling and possessive. "Girl, go play with the kids outside and leave your momma alone."

Those words hurt me. I wanted to spend time with my mother but I couldn't. During this time, my mother was totally wrapped up with Toots, leaving no time for me and my siblings. My oldest brother would often talk back at Toots for screaming at me. All this bothered me, but because I remained in Toots' house, I realized I had to listen to his directions.

Things escalated. Every night my mother would get drunk, fuss, and fight. The police came to our apartment at least two to three times per week. As a child, I just wanted my life to get better. I got tired of seeing vodka bottles, Bacardi Rum, cigarettes, and beer in an apartment full of alcoholic adults. I also became tired of Toots screaming, hitting, and threatening my mother.

When my mother was drunk from Private Stock beer and Old English 800, I always knew an argument would begin. Toots was very controlling, but once my mother became intoxicated, she refused to follow his commands. When my mother would not follow his commands, he would scream at her, "BITCH, I TOOK YOU AND YOUR KIDS INTO MY HOUSE, AND YOU ARE GOING TO DO WHAT I SAY!"

My mother would stand up to him—all 85 pounds of her—and threaten to harm him with the telephone. On one occasion she threatened to kill him with a knife. I was hysterical, and the only thing I knew how to do was to call 911. I remember screaming and crying, "COME ON, MOMMIE! LET'S LEAVE!"—while I prayed to get away from this man.

Sometimes we would leave and stay with my godmother in the Bronx. But then we returned to Toots' house. He would be nice for a few days, and then he would become controlling, hateful, and mean once again.

I often prayed, GOD, LET US MOVE SOUTH TO A BETTER PLACE. Every summer we had visited my grandparents in Greenville, NC. It was peaceful, quiet, clean, and stable. My brothers and I were supervised more. I would play jump rope with my cousin. We'd go to the mall. We'd go to church. We'd cook. I'd ride with my grandfather in his truck, while he took care of his landscaping business.

But we didn't move. And as I watched things unfold, I had a feeling that the old addicted mother was emerging. My mother and Toots would leave me and my siblings unattended. When it was time for school the next morning, my mother was nowhere to be found. I had to prepare on my own, including fixing my hair and getting something to eat. I learned to care for myself at an early age.

Soon I realized my perception was right, except this time, my mother began to shoot heroin, and Toots would administer the shots. He would make us go outside and play, while he would shoot heroin needles into my mother's arm and leg. I would come back from playing, only to see my mother's arm and leg swollen and covered with circles.

I hated Toots and became very defiant towards him. He never talked to my brothers ugly, because they could physically hurt him, but Toots would berate me when he knew that my brothers were not around. I started sleeping with a knife under my bed. The stress kept building inside of me. The verbal abuse continued. One time Toots told me, "YOUR MOMMA AIN'T SHIT, AND YOU AIN'T GONNA BE SHIT."

Those words really hurt.

In November 1987, on a rainy day, two social workers from the New York City Department of Child Protective Services came to Toots' apartment requesting my siblings and me into their care. The adults lied and said that we did not stay at that address. When the social workers left, I cried and hollered because I did not want my siblings and me to go into foster care. OH NO, I thought, WE ARE GOING TO BE SEPARATED, AND I WILL NEVER BE ABLE TO SEE MY BROTHERS AGAIN. I cared deeply about my brothers. They were my safety net.

On another night Toots and my mother had gotten into an argument in Harlem. As usual, my mother was drunk. My brothers were staying with my grandmother because they were tired of Toots, but I had to stay behind. I don't remember what the fight was about, but Toots hit my mother outside of my aunt's apartment complex and when he hit my mother, I immediately picked up a trashcan and hit him, causing him to fall on the concrete. "YOU ONE LEG BASTARD!" I screamed. "YOU WILL NEVER TOUCH MY MOTHER AGAIN!"

I ran into the apartment and made my aunt call 911. That was the last time I ever saw Toots. At the tender age of 7, I had learned how to protect myself.

Shortly after that, my mother decided to move South. The lifestyle of dysfunction ended when she chose to relocate from New York City to North Carolina on January 16, 1988.

I am proud to say that my mother has been free from the lifestyle of addiction for 19 years. As a family, we found refuge in the church. My mother went back to college and graduated with her associate's degree in criminal justice. We attended family therapy to work through the issues of neglect, abandonment, and grief, and we were able to mend the broken pieces. My family is doing extremely well.

At a very young age, I learned the power of imagination. I had to imagine the life I wanted to live. The power of my imagination brought forth reality. As an adult, I continue to use imagination in every area of my life. Growing up in a single-parent home, I had to learn how to wait on everything I desired. In the midst of chaos and confusion, as a child I cried a lot. Through my experiences, I know the meaning of having a good cry.

Crying represents freedom, cleansing, and healing. Sometimes, I have had to let my emotions out by crying. When I cry over some of my past hurts, my soul opens up to the virtue of healing. Crying allows a person to be real with themselves. If a person is feeling frustrated, angry, or worried, I would encourage them to have a good cry. Iyanla Vanzant describes a good cry as your nose running, ears being hot, head hurting really badly, and having a pile of soiled tissues. When I grasped this concept back in 2005, healing occurred in my life. Because of this poem, my life will never be the same.

This poem speaks of the pain of the past, which does not have to be today's reality. The writer endured emotional abuse, teen pregnancy, poverty, and emotional breakdown. Through these great trials, she emerged a winner. Therefore, I tell myself through my obstacles in life, I am going to be a winner, despite generational misprints of the past—the chaos, confusion, and instability brought upon me at an early age. I will be a champion at everything I try to accomplish.

As a future school counselor, I know that I possess the awareness, understanding, and empathy to help children experiencing grief, abandonment, and neglect. Shaped by my past experiences, I will be a beacon of light and hope to encourage students that they can succeed through any challenge.

* * *

SCHEFT'S RESPONSE

One of the techniques Taheera uses in the piece is providing her inner thoughts. As I noted in the first chapter, this is a dramatic, insightful device that adds immediacy and intimacy.

Most students I teach have never been taught the technique, let alone its value. When I recommend it, most students find it very easy to do. I offer the following written instructions in terms of graphic considerations:

When you express your inner thoughts, remember not to use quotation marks, which are for the stuff that comes out of one's mouth. However, when you write thoughts, they may lack graphic impact.

What a jerk, I thought.

So you can try variations—like italics or a different font. Make sure you're consistent.

What a jerk , I thought.

I like to do something I've seen Tom (not Thomas) Wolfe do—use all CAPITAL letters for thoughts:

WHAT A JERK, I thought.

It's very graphic and easy for the reader to follow. It's so clear that after you've established it, you can leave off the "I thought's." Example:

"Excuse me, sir," I said. THAT'S RIGHT. PRETEND I'M NOT HERE, I thought. "Excuse me."

"Yes? May I help you."

NO, I'M JUST STANDING HERE WAITING FOR A BUS. "Yes, sir, I wanted to talk with you about my last paper." THE ONE YOU GAVE ME A "D" ON, YOU JERK.

If there are too many thoughts packed together, some people feel it's hard to keep the points straight, but you can deal with that by interspersing thoughts with dialogue and action/detail. Example:

David sits on the bench and pounds his right fist into his baseball glove. "Come on, Ralph. Strike 'im out." *I hate sitting here game after game. Only reason Billy's in is because he's the coach's son.* "Nice one, Ralph. You got 'im."

David looks over at the coach. *He never gives me a chance. Never.* He looks away, then turns his hat around backwards. *I definitely wouldn't have struck out like Kenny in the last game. I can hit. Everybody knows that.*

CHAPTER 14

FLYING LESSONS

Amanda Riley Smith

Editor's Note: Amanda Riley Smith, a former United Methodist minister, has found her second calling in the classroom as an educator. She enjoys teaching students at Brogden Middle School in Durham, NC. In summer 2007, she was fortunate to work with the children at John Avery Boys and Girls Club in Durham.

Amanda is also a graduate student in the Master of Teaching in Special Education Program at North Carolina Central University. She loves reading and works at Borders Bookstore in Chapel Hill. In addition to reading, Amanda writes and always finds time to spend with friends and with her dog, Mollie.

* * *

FLYING LESSONS

When you have come to the end of all the light you know, and you are about to step into the darkness of the unknown, faith is knowing one of two things will happen: you will be given something solid to stand on or you will be taught how to fly.

—Source Unknown

Inspiring Student Writers: Strategies and Examples for Teachers
pp. 123–128
Copyright © 2009 by Information Age Publishing

This quote captures how I feel about my life and about the lives of others around me. It speaks to what I fear and what I worry about the most: the unknown. A friend handed me this quote about 10 years ago. Little did I know at the time, but the words written on this small, crinkled piece of paper would sustain me throughout the following years. At different times, the "darkness of the unknown," "something solid to stand on," and "being taught how to fly" have taken on different definitions; however, the overall meaning of the quote has stayed the same: I will be okay, and even thrive, amidst the unknown changes in my life.

A life-changing turning point occurred 1 and one-half years ago when a committee of the church eliminated my position as Minister of Education and Pastoral Care. (This decision was not in any way due to my job performance.) The committee planned this staff restructuring for a few months but did not tell me until the evening it became effective. Within one hour, I had lost my job, my income, my career, my confidence and, ultimately, my calling.

All of my theological preparation, education, and dedication to the church seemed to be whisked away in one moment. This point was definitely the "end of all the light" I had ever known. Church had been the center of my life for as long as I could remember. More than that, I had spent one-third of my life as a minister. Abandoned by the church, I turned to any source of comfort I could find. I felt alone, empty, and in the midst of a terrible darkness of the unknown.

After a month, I was given "something solid to stand on"—a job as a teacher assistant of children with autism at an elementary school. Although I had never imagined myself out of the pulpit, I traded my ministerial robe for jeans and a t-shirt, my stole for a school nametag, my sermons for lesson plans, and a sanctuary for a classroom.

Initially, I believed that this job was just a place to rest for a time and to receive a paycheck, albeit a small one. After the first week, I wanted to resign several times, but I continued to have faith. As the school year unfolded, I began to realize that teaching these children and children like them is my new and unexpected calling. I had traded much more than the things in my ministerial life; I had traded my darkness for light. I had been taught to fly and these children helped me soar beyond the circumstances that led me to them.

The message of this quote also transfers into my teaching life. Each day is a small venture into the unknown, for me and for the children. Because the children have autism, often one cannot predict how their behavior will change from day to day. I find that sometimes the best plan is to plan to be flexible with the plans. As someone who likes predictability, I have found the faith to know that I will deal effectively with the children's variability.

These children also desire and thrive on predictability and routine. They, also, become anxious when confronted with the unknown. Part of my job is to instill in them the faith that they will be okay when the unpredictable, the unknown, occurs. I want them to understand that they will be given something to stand on or will be taught how to deal effectively and rise above the current circumstances.

One child, in particular, helped me navigate my way through the darkness into the light of teaching. Jerry, an African American, 8-year-old boy who preferred to be called "SpongeBob," came to the school about the same time I did. New to the class, neither of us knew anyone. Other teachers told me, "You will not be able to understand Jerry's speech. There is little hope for him. He will never leave this classroom. And he will never learn to read." Hearing this despair made me want to help Jerry even more.

I'll admit, sometimes working with Jerry was challenging, but I found him to be charming. Every morning he arrived at school wearing a freshly ironed button-down shirt tucked in to his jeans, which had been pressed so much that they could stand on their own. Talking almost constantly, he wanted to communicate and be connected to people. I believed him to be smart in so many ways. He could take an ordinary object and make almost anything out of it: a ruler became a barber's tool; a ring became a basketball hoop; a calculator became a cell phone; a staple became a toy animal's earring; bricks became a block party.

As the year went on, I learned how to "speak Jerry." I could understand his speech and then could relate it to other teachers. The things that he said were pretty funny too. I taught him how to play tag on the playground and would only push him on the swings if he said the alphabet and counted to 50. Both of us moved from darkness to light.

And then, both of us began to soar. Jerry was mainstreamed for art, music and media. In October, he participated in a musical called "Spaced Out" with the other third graders. He sang the songs and did the choreography. As I sat backstage, I watched him singing only a few feet away from me. His eyes glistened in the spotlights as he clapped his hands to the rhythm and pointed upward. He looked over at me and sang, "Blast off on a great adventure! Blast off, we're gonna fly. Blast off to the moon and planets. We're taking off to the sky!"

With my own eyes glistening with tears, I thought, *Yes, Jerry, we ARE gonna fly.*

Several days later, Jerry read for the first time. In another week, he sat on the sofa with his feet propped up and read a book to himself. I heard whispers as he went through each sentence, only stopping enough to say, "Misssmith, what this word says?"

Jerry was soaring, and so was I. As I watched him read, I heard his sweet singing voice in my mind, "We're taking off to the sky!"

As I become a special education teacher, I suspect I will lean on the message of this quote many times. The unknown will always be present, but so will my faith. Let the flying lessons continue!

*   *   *

SCHEFT'S RESPONSE

This should come as no surprise, but in the first version of this paper there was no Jerry example. Most students—most people—I know are reluctant to talk about the great things they do. "You want me to brag?" they ask me. It's a rhetorical question, meaning: "What's wrong with you?" And then I say, "No. Give me a success story to illustrate your point."

It's not easy for educators to write about being great. Sometimes it takes a few drafts and a little judicious, relentless pushing, pushing, pushing from me, but when it's finished, it makes sense. And the authors realize that telling the truth isn't bragging. It's good writing. Again, what I'm talking about is SHOWING, not just telling.

When I read Amanda's piece, I was struck with her description of teaching as a "calling." I'd heard teachers use the term before, but this was the first time I heard a member of the clergy use it to describe working in the classroom.

In the piece she talks about her initial pursuit of teaching as "just a place to rest for a time and to receive a paycheck, albeit a small one." That's a common presumption—which plays itself out constantly. Teaching is a hard gig, and many leave because it is so difficult. As Amanda wrote, "[a]fter the first week, I wanted to resign several times." That's common too. I say to my students all the time, "A lot of people out there think you're idiots for wanting to be teachers. They think you're saps working for the small paycheck. And they think just about anybody can do what you want to do. To them, teaching is babysitting. Of course most of them couldn't do the job. They wouldn't last until lunchtime ... let alone the first hour."

So what makes Amanda stay? Faith. And that belief is answered. Of course it doesn't always happen this way for educators, but Amanda's paper makes clear the unique riches the job can provide.

Reading her paper also reminded me of a fantastic poem:

WHAT TEACHERS MAKE, OR
OBJECTION OVERRULED, OR
IF THINGS DON'T WORK OUT,
YOU CAN ALWAYS GO TO LAW SCHOOL
By Taylor Mali

He says the problem with teachers is, "What's a kid going to learn
from someone who decided his best option in life was to become a teacher?"
He reminds the other dinner guests that it's true what they say about
teachers:
Those who can, do; those who can't, teach.

I decide to bite my tongue instead of his
and resist the temptation to remind the other dinner guests
that it's also true what they say about lawyers.

Because we're eating, after all, and this is polite company.

"I mean, you're a teacher, Taylor," he says.
"Be honest. What do you make?"

And I wish he hadn't done that
(asked me to be honest)
because, you see, I have a policy
about honesty and ass-kicking:
if you ask for it, I have to let you have it.

You want to know what I make?

I make kids work harder than they ever thought they could.
I can make a C+ feel like a Congressional medal of honor
and an A- feel like a slap in the face.
How dare you waste my time with anything less than your very best.
I make kids sit through 40 minutes of study hall
in absolute silence. No, you may not work in groups.
No, you may not ask a question.
Why won't I let you get a drink of water?
Because you're not thirsty, you're bored, that's why.

I make parents tremble in fear when I call home:
I hope I haven't called at a bad time,
I just wanted to talk to you about something Billy said today.
Billy said, "Leave the kid alone. I still cry sometimes, don't you?"
And it was the noblest act of courage I have ever seen.

I make parents see their children for who they are
and what they can be.

You want to know what I make?
I make kids wonder,
I make them question.
I make them criticize.
I make them apologize and mean it.
I make them write, write, write.
And then I make them read.
I make them spell definitely beautiful, definitely beautiful, definitely
beautiful
over and over and over again until they will never misspell
either one of those words again.
I make them show all their work in math.
And hide it on their final drafts in English.
I make them understand that if you got this (brains)
then you follow this (heart) and if someone ever tries to judge you
by what you make, you give them this (the finger).

Let me break it down for you, so you know what I say is true:

I make a goddamn difference! What about you?

Taylor Mali is a former teacher and classically trained actor who now makes his living as a professional poet. One of the original poets to appear on the HBO series *Russell Simmons Presents Def Poetry,* he is a veteran of the poetry slam and the author of *What Learning Leaves* and several spoken word CDs and DVDs. He lives and writes in New York City. For more information, visit www.taylormali.com.

CHAPTER 15

THE POWER
OF UNCONDITIONAL LOVE

Elwood L. Robinson

Editor's Note: Elwood L. Robinson is dean of the College of Behavioral
and Social Sciences at North Carolina Central University. A clinical psychologist, he has taught for over 20 years, specializing in the treatment of
depression and anxiety disorders. His research interests include psychoso-
cial factors related to cardiovascular disease and cancer.

A retired morning pick-up basketball player after 20 years, Elwood is now
a spinning (biking) enthusiast, leaving behind a stellar career and "the
sweetest jump shot this side of the legendary 'Big O' Oscar Robertson."

* * *

SCHEFT'S INTRODUCTION

I was a little surprised by Elwood's biographical statement. Kinda brief.
He could have easily written more; he's an accomplished individual. That
he chose to be so sparse tells you something about the man.

I've known Elwood for a number of years. He is one of the "stars" at
NCCU—a respected researcher, a dynamic teacher, and an all-around
great guy, able to be "at home" with anyone from chancellors to deans to

Inspiring Student Writers: Strategies and Examples for Teachers
pp. 129–136

trustees to politicians to parents to students. I discuss linguistic plurality in this book's appendix, and Elwood is a master of the technique—comfortable in discussing erudite research matters, sports, politics, or the latest in popular culture. He is immediately likeable and engaging. As a matter of fact, I'd describe him as charismatic—a word I'm usually hesitant to use. He is, without a doubt, one of the most confident people I know, but it is based on genuineness and earnestness, not arrogance.

Elwood is also a very straightforward, honest person—unafraid to open up to a group and express his feelings, make himself vulnerable, step out from his usual persona as somebody totally "together" and in absolute control. This willingness to be "real" is clearly a part of why people gravitate to him—to seek his counsel or just "hang" with him.

Elwood's values are infused in his conversation, although it's subtle; he's not a "preacher." While a gifted speaker, he is someone who leads by example, through actions more than words. He credits much of his success to his parents. It is hard for him to explain this in words, but he makes the attempt in the following piece. He focuses on his father, which he did earlier in "Wednesdays and Sundays," an article included in Tavis Smiley's *Keeping the Faith: Stories of Love, Courage, Healing, and Hope From Black America*.

In that piece Elwood talks about his weekly visits to his father. From his home in Durham, NC, he would drive 90 minutes to Clinton, grocery shop for his aunt and mother, then visit his father at the nursing home. He'd transport his dad to the family home. "My father was in a wheelchair and often sick and fragile, so just getting him in and out of my car was an adventure," said Elwood. "Bathroom issues were part of the 30-mile drive. When we arrived at our home in Ivanhoe, I had to get him into the house and make sure he was comfortable. We'd spend about 5 hours visiting in his home. During that time, I had to help with additional bathroom experiences. Then I'd get him back in the car for the return trip."

Elwood followed this routine every Sunday for 9 years.

* * *

THE POWER OF UNCONDITIONAL LOVE

What is the source of motivation and the special essence that makes life meaningful? This question has led me to reflect on the forces that enable us to be successful in achieving our life's goals and aspirations. These existential streams of consciousness are often accompanied by thoughts of the role that our developmental preparation plays in how we approach and have impact on the world. I believe that our preparation for success begins very early in life—starting with social needs, particularly love and trust, which are paramount in allowing us to negotiate a successful and satisfying life.

Abraham Maslow, a psychologist, developed a theory of human development that is based on needs. This theory, known as Maslow's Hierarchy of Needs, suggests that embedded in the very nature of each human being are certain needs that must be attained in order for a person to be whole physically, psychologically, and emotionally. First, there are physiological needs—oxygen, water, food, and other minerals. Second are safety and security needs, and the need for protection. Third is the need for love and belonging, manifest in the drive to establish affectionate relationships or create a sense of community. Fourth are the esteem needs, which Maslow divides into two parts—respect of others and self-respect. The fifth and final stage forms the pinnacle and is identified as self-actualization or the desire for self-fulfillment, to become everything one is capable of becoming.

According to Maslow's theory, the order in which these needs appear in the hierarchy is the order in which humans must attain them. Needs higher in the hierarchy cannot be attained without first satisfying the more basic needs at the base. When any level of these needs is not met, a deficit need is created, causing a negative effect on human psychology.

While Maslow has his critics, his theory explains a great deal about human development. However, it does not explain how individuals who are born with limited resources or in poverty are able to have a successful development. I grew up in rural North Carolina in some of the worst poverty conditions imaginable.

I was raised in a house that had no central air conditioning or heat. It would have been condemned by most authorities in the civilized world. There was no running water or bathroom to be found in the house or nearby surroundings. The nearest facility was 50 yards east of the house, known affectionately as an "outhouse." Imagine what it was like to have to "go" in the middle of the night in the dead of winter. The house was a dilapidated structure with cracks in the walls and in the floor. I could lie in bed and see the ground beneath the house. In the summer, I'd often gaze down through the floorboards to view a few of the chickens that had taken respite from the blistering heat.

I imagine it would be easy for someone to read that last paragraph and think, *Wow. That's sad.* But I never felt that way. Growing up, I thought my life was great. In spite of horrible physical conditions and limited resources, my parents compensated with massive amounts of love, respect, trust, and compassion. My father did not leave me a trust fund, a family business, or an estate. He left me something more valuable. He left me a special and everlasting memory that he loved me unconditionally. This wonderful gift is one I hope to give to others.

I need to tell you a little about my father. He was a small man, about 5'6" and 150 pounds, and he spent most of his life working very hard. He farmed a small area of land outside our home, raising tobacco and corn, but most of the time he cut timber in Sampson County. Most everybody recognized my dad's yellow Ford truck, and they were amazed that this diminutive, yet extremely strong man worked by himself, rather than in the typical arrangement of two-to-three people. He would cut down trees—usually pine or oak—trim off the branches and cut them into 6-to-8-foot sections. He'd move the limbs to a scrap pile. Then he'd haul the logs and stack them in his truck—filling the 15 x 6-foot bed and piling the logs as high as 8 feet. He'd secure the load with chains, and then drive to the processing plant.

Moving and stacking the logs was an arduous task. He would lift up one end of a log, then tip it up on his shoulder, and as though he were a soldier carrying a rifle, walk to the truck, flip the log onto the bed, and return to repeat the process. He would spend *hours* doing this. You couldn't tell this from looking at him clothed, but with his shirt off, my father had huge knots on his shoulders. Occasionally, beginning when I was 12 years old, I would help him stack logs, and I learned a very important lesson: I did not want to do this for a living.

Again, you may be thinking: *Poor you.* I never felt that way, and I don't believe my dad ever felt that way. I never heard him complain. He seemed very content with his life. He used to get so much pleasure from little things—a new shirt, a new tie. If you bought my dad something, he had it on in no longer than 20 minutes. He never talked much, but you could tell when he was happy, and it was usually over little things—like going to a baseball game, fishing at Jones Lake or White Lake. When I graduated from college, I bought him a new suit; he really liked that suit. Another time, when I told him I wanted him to be the best man at my wedding, I said, "We'll need to wear tuxedos." I could tell his reaction from his eyes. "Tuxedos," he said. Later, as I was walking away, I heard him say, "*Tuxedos.*"

All through my childhood my parents gave me the gift of unconditional love. They almost never lectured me, but they sent me "messages" all the time. We had this connection. They treated me as an individual. They gave me independence and power. I had tremendous freedom—to go and do, to play, to learn. There were very few constraints. I never had a curfew.

Now some children might have taken advantage of this situation. I didn't. And although they never told me *directly* that I needed to consider them, I got that message. And although they never talked *directly* about trust, they offered it to me early in my life. Because of how they lived, because of their example, because of all the things they gave me, I learned to be responsible. I knew I had to figure out certain things for myself. I knew I needed to do the right thing. And while they never said it aloud, I heard their message: "We trust you to do the right thing." And while they never said it aloud, I heard other messages through their example: "There is value in working." "Provide for your family." "Treat people well."

Unconditional love—this gift became evident during the nine years that my father lived in a nursing home. I visited him weekly. My visits seemed to be the most important part of his week. In fact, these visits seemed to provide a kind of therapy that sustained and gave him strength to make it through the next week. I truly believe my visits and our relationship added several years to his life. Each time I entered the room, his eyes would light up, and he was energized and empowered by my visit. If you've been to nursing homes, you know how much a person's eyes convey about how they feel. This was more than my father appearing happy. At that moment, through his eyes, we became connected.

The nursing staff constantly told me that my father was very proud and often talked about me during the week. Each member of the staff had an inside track on my life, because after each visit, my father spent the rest of the week talking to them about me and my life. He never asked or wanted me to bring him anything. He just wanted to see his son. I was proud to be his son and thankful that my presence was therapeutic for a dying father.

My father and I had a ritual that became a staple of our visits. He was always in his wheelchair, rolling around the nursing center talking to someone. I would sneak up behind him, give him a big hug, and whisper:

Behold, how good and how pleasant it is
For brethren to dwell together in unity!
It is like the precious ointment upon the head,
That ran down upon the beard,
Even Aaron's beard:
That went down to the skirts of his garments;
As the dew of Hermon,
And as the dew that descended upon the mountains of Zion;
For there the Lord commanded the blessing,
Even life for evermore. (Psalms 133)

Recently, events in my life, taking care of my disabled parents, and several conversations I have had with my students have caused me to think that Maslow may have underestimated the need for love, particularly in the early stages of development. I believe that love and unconditional love are the most important contributions anyone can make to the well-being of an individual.

"Unconditional Love" was the second posthumous single released by Tupac Shakur from his greatest hits album. The lyrics of this song are consistent with my thinking. Tupac speaks of unconditional love as "the stuff that don't wear off" and "don't fade." It is a love that endures, lasting "all these crazy days [and] these crazy nights." It is a love that goes beyond notions of right and wrong, a love that is dependable, always there "no matter what," always there in the heart.

Unconditional love is a gift without any strings attached. No invoice is ever written. No charge is ever made. It arrives without asking, delivered on a breeze—so softly sent that it can go unnoticed, as if it didn't exist. Unconditional love seeks no reward, no response, and no glory for its gift. To experience it is truly something special. It is the fuel that sustains passion. Those who receive it are blessed with the preparation that enables them to appreciate life and its vicissitudes. I am thankful that my parents gave me this gift.

The personification of love is seen in unique ways. One moment came for me when I witnessed the birth of my daughter almost 22 years ago. Her birth stands as the most significant and defining moment of my life. The moment I saw the "crown" of her head it was love at first sight. I am thankful for the opportunity to have been by my wife's side, as she and I fell in love again together. That moment gave us a precious example of how we could experience love at a deeper and more profound level. I would repeat this moment again, some eight years later, with the birth of my son. There is nothing that can compare, nothing that comes close to the love a parent feels for his or her child.

My son is very special, because it is through him that I can see the extension of my father and me. I am blessed to have him in my life. I jokingly tell him often that he is my "favorite son." To this he replies, "Dad, I am your only son."

I read somewhere that God never takes those things from you that you truly love; she just replaces them. My message here is that persons who die are not taken away; their essence is transformed. I have been privileged to see this following the death of my father. My son is an extension of my father. Everyday his physical appearance, temperament, and personality remind me of my father. I hope and pray that I have been able to give the gift my father gave me—bonding built on shared love and joy. I enjoy my children's company immensely.

I do not expect my children to love me back as fiercely as I love them. I don't expect them to be grateful to me, to take care of me, or to be considerate of what I want or need. I do not want them to take care of me when I am old or senile. It would be nice to have these extra bonuses in our relationship, but I by no means expect it. But I believe those who have been the recipients of unconditional love will be compelled to give it to others. Therefore, I fully expect that my children will provide these amenities without conditions. I believe they understand that I will always love them, and they can't do anything to change how I feel about them. I want my children to pass on the gift of unconditional love to their children.

The twilight of life is that moment when life and death share the same space. It is during this period that we believe people think about their life's value and purpose. I have no idea what will be the status of my physical or emotional well-being. However, I predict that two things will happen. One, I will be extremely proud and grateful for having the opportunity to share my time with everyone on the planet. Two, that the love that my parents, Isaiah and Hannah Robinson, gave to me that I passed on to my children will make the transition from life to death extremely rewarding and peaceful.

*   *   *

SCHEFT'S RESPONSE

Writing about the people we love is not easy. I remember—decades ago—when I was applying to college, one application required an essay about the person you admire most. I didn't have to stop and think. I'd write about my dad.

And I began.

And I couldn't do it. Everything I wanted to say … I just couldn't find the right words. Everything I wrote was terrible—disturbingly clichéd and trivial. I knew my feelings were right, strong. But, as the saying goes, I couldn't put them into words. I struggled with this for days. I got frustrated, then angry, then embarrassed. This man who had given me so much, who had been such a hard working, positive, kind example … why couldn't I communicate that to any meaningful degree?

I finally gave up. I don't remember what I ended up using for the essay, but it certainly wasn't what I wanted to say. Eventually, though, I came to understand the experience not as a failure, but as the realization that there are some things in life—people and events, good and true and important—that we may not be able to render in words.

Elwood's piece does a fine job of communicating the elusive quality of unconditional love. Much that he communicates hides "between the lines." Writing his article was not an easy task for him. The paper went through several drafts. On one occasion I just listened to Elwood talk about his father, while I made some notes. That led to a new version.

Again, I go back to the writing process and the writer's quest to make her/his work better. We are so often tempted to give up. I'M EXHAUSTED, we think. THIS IS TOO HARD, TOO PAINFUL, TOO FRUSTRATING. IT'S GOOD ENOUGH. Fortunately, we usually know when we're kidding ourselves—that we need to hang in there, to write, to polish, and maybe write some more ... just a little bit more.

CHAPTER 16

TESTING THE SLEEPING GIANT

Pamela George

Editor's Note: Pamela George is an educator, artist, and author. After serving as an educational psychology professor at NCCU for nearly 3 decades, she recently opened a painting studio in Durham, North Carolina.

Her professional assignments have taken her to many exotic places—Samoa (as a Peace Corps teacher), Thailand, Portugal, the Maldives (as a Fulbright Professor), China, Hong Kong and Southeast Asia (as a film-maker), and most recently South Africa (as a Senior Fulbright Specialist).

George is the artist and designer of *The North Carolina Alphabet* (Carolina Wren Press), which celebrates the state's outdoor life. Her paintings (including recent work on the Maldives, as a National Park Artist in Residency, and from her alphabet book) can be seen on her Web site: www.pamelageorge.net.

* * *

SCHEFT INTRODUCTION

When I think of Pamela, I'm reminded of a song Peggy Lee used to sing, "I'm a Woman." Basically, the gal can do just about anything, and what she does she does great. Period. She is a master teacher, researcher, documentary filmmaker, carpenter, writer, artist ... and whatever else she sets her mind to. An astounding combination of science, alchemy, and artistry,

Inspiring Student Writers: Strategies and Examples for Teachers
pp. 137–141

she is the closest person I know to TV's MacGyver. I believe if given a few materials (e.g., string, a sea urchin, chewing gum, and duct tape)—she could make, fix, and/or improve just about anything.

Pamela is politically astute and an activist for a number of causes and concerns. Like many who work for change, she is an educator first. She tries to teach, to help people. She doesn't intimidate, inflame, or embarrass. Through her travels all over the world, she was teaching about multiculturalism and diversity decades before these terms were thrust on the public consciousness. Her mission has been and continues to be cultural awareness and sensitivity—not only stressing our differences but highlighting our similarities.

Upon meeting Pamela, one finds her immediately charming, humorous, serious, and respectful. What is not readily apparent is her constant, passionate drive to live a productive life, respect people, and do the right thing. I can't totally explain it, but I suspect her success has something to do with her Louisiana childhood and, in the course of a lifetime, her consumption of gallons (and gallons) of hot sauce.

The following piece differs a bit from the book's other examples. It's not a reflection stemming from an inspirational source. However, it makes an important contribution by illustrating certain qualities found in many of the best educators. How many of us, upon seeing a problem, pretend it's not there? When we're told thre is no recourse to a given dilemma, how many of us welcome the chance to stop, to give in, to give up?

Except for the author and her daughter, the names of the characters have been changed.

* * *

TESTING THE SLEEPING GIANT

My daughter, Kemen, has always liked math. She breezed through homework, tutored other kids in her elementary classes, and mastered an advanced calculator early. But at the end of third grade on her standardized end-of-grade test scores in math, she scored in the *sixth* percentile— ranking at the bottom of her class.

Such a low score was a blow to her confidence. It meant that she would be passed over for special classes for academically gifted students and, in some systems, would have been retained. Because I knew Kemen was very accomplished in elementary math, I began to search out the cause of such a faulty test result. I asked to view the exam and, when denied, I asked for a retest—also denied. I then persisted that her original test be scored by hand.

It was discovered that the score sheet she was given for her exam had been a photocopy, presumably made when the test proctors ran out of originals. The scoring machine could not accurately read the photocopied score sheet, yet it did not flag the test. Rather, it reported a false, low score.

Today Kemen is a proud young woman who, skilled and rewarded in her high school advanced math classes, has completed her graduate studies in environmental science and is a wiz in applied math and statistics. But this experience with my daughter's third grade math score would shape my work for years to come.

For most of my adult life, my *job* was being a college teacher, but my *work* went beyond that job. As a professor of educational psychology for nearly 3 decades, my dream has always been to teach in a world where students are judged by their actual performances, where standardized tests are few and fair, and where test scores are only a small, modest part of students' educational records. My charge has been to train teachers, counselors and principals to evaluate students and school programs with authentic assessments that are less harmful to kids than single standardized IQ and other aptitude or achievement tests.

After the experience with my own daughter, my righteous anger grew, and I began to counsel other parents whose children were erroneously labeled as mentally retarded based on IQ test scores. I worked with teachers whose good judgments concerning students were often trumped by standardized tests. I observed classes where "drill and kill" test preparation became the curriculum. As a college teacher, I advised many students whose educational futures had been eclipsed by standardized test scores that clearly underrepresented their capabilities. For example, Keisha had been passed over for placement in a teacher education program at the state's flagship university, and William was rejected from a graduate counseling program for which he would have been remarkably well suited.

My indignation toward the misuse and overuse of standardized testing was fueled by geography. I work in the South, the region that has led the vanguard in testing children. Though other regions would follow, it was the first area in the nation to require kindergarten ready-or-not testing, first and second grade testing, grade-retention based on test scores, high school competency testing, and so on. The testing business burgeoned. Testing and publishing companies were selling millions of standardized tests to state departments of public instruction, school boards, and legislatures.

Based on my work with parents, teachers and students, and with the support of a small foundation grant, I wrote a book called *Testing Our Children*—one of the first of what would later become a popular trend in consumer-oriented books calling for test reform. A readable text with testing psychometrics simplified and test questions demystified, my book steered parents and teachers to published records of court cases where specific test items were contested when they were used for placing children into special education programs.

It is well documented that many minority children in the South have been erroneously labeled as mentally handicapped using IQ test scores as the defining criteria. My book illustrated common errors in test items and testing practices, and it taught parents about their rights in testing and test-use situations. The book was reviewed favorably in the education media and regional press. As I had expected, primarily because there were few test resources for students or parents at the time, the book was popular and the first edition was soon sold out. Just when I thought the path of my work was clear and justice had been served, a sleeping giant woke.

One of the country's wealthiest test companies brought legal action against me for *Testing Our Children*. As publisher of a commonly used IQ test, it claimed my book, by telling readers the source of specific test items hitherto kept confidential from parents and teachers, encouraged parents to violate the company's copyright laws. In addition to claims of enormous financial damages, they demanded that my book's sales be stopped and that I never write, teach, or lecture about standardized testing again.

The language of the company's New York lawyers stunned me, for I am by nature polite and pacifistic. The vehemence with which they pursued me frightened me, for I did not have tenure at my university and this action would surely jeopardize the prospects. The company's demand for financial reparations astounded me, for it represented more money than I or my whole family could earn in a lifetime.

As an educational psychologist whose work was advocating for fair and open testing, what was I to do? If I capitulated to the industry's legal pit bulls, I would certainly lose my *work*, which provided meaning and a sense of "calling" beyond a job. But if I fought back, I would most likely lose my *job*—a professorship for which I had worked hard, earned a PhD, but did not yet have tenure.

Consumed by my dilemma, for a few days I didn't eat anything. A friend called me "trauma trim." For several nights I didn't sleep beyond nodding. I tossed and turned in doubt and self-loathing. *Why did this happen to me when I had the best of intentions?* I wondered. *Who among my readers would have been so unkind to report my efforts to the test company?* I raged, *How could I have been so egotistical, so sanctimonious, so stupid to believe there wouldn't be a price to pay?*

Then, when I was in the darkest and most frightening cave of this predicament, I had a profound awareness: I was *not* in this situation alone. For several years prior to this battle with the test company, I had met or corresponded with colleagues around the country who had shared my concerns about the misuse of standardized tests. There had developed a loose coalition of like-minded educators and civil-rights advocates across the country—from Sacramento, California to Boston, Massachusetts— who worked on test reform. I called a few of these colleagues who each called a few more.

Soon the news of my situation began to reverberate. Bob, a colleague and a public relations wizard, crafted an explanation of my situation, which we used to rally this informal alliance:

> The large testing industry is trying to set some insidious legal precedent for copyright superiority by beating up on a well-meaning teacher from a public university in the South who is unlikely to fight back.

By the end of the second day, messages of support were flooding in from coast to coast—from Ted, a local journalism school professor; Page, a rural educator; John, a national test reform advocate; Diana, a lawyer experienced in test litigation; and many others.

By the end of the week, an education advocacy center based at Harvard began to coordinate my defense. Soon a famous law firm in Washington, D.C., took the case pro bono. This team of lawyers chose to fight, using the First Amendment's safeguarding of the right of a teacher or parent to criticize test materials and practices. My courage grew with my confidence that the work I was doing was important, necessary, and well supported. We settled this legal case favorably out of court in a few months. The book again was available for sale, and my continued work and criticism of the inappropriate use of standardized testing was allowed.

One day near the end of the deliberations, I remember looking around the Washington conference room at the group of powerful advocates from Boston, New York, and D.C. and the bevy of colleagues (now friends) who championed *Testing Our Children* and shared my dream of better assessment measures for kids. I felt so grateful for their support, their knowledge, their skills, and their energy. And I realized that the testing industry had picked on the *wrong* woman!

APPENDIX

CHAPTER 17

CONFRONTING STEREOTYPING

Understanding Why We Do It, Considering What to Do About It

Tom Scheft

"I don't like Jews," said my 9-year-old sister quite matter of factly. Right smack in the middle of Sunday lunch. The year was 1960.

My family—mother, father, six children—was seated around the dining room table. I was 11, the oldest of the kids.

After my sister's pronouncement, I immediately looked at my mother. Her face was momentarily blank, followed briefly by a startled expression. She stiffened slightly, regained her composure, then turned toward her daughter with a forced, frozen smile. "What do you mean?" she asked calmly.

My sister, who had resumed eating, stopped and looked up at our mother. "I don't like Jews," she repeated, again quite conversationally— the way a fourth grader might casually "put down" someone in her class. ("I don't like Greg. He thinks he's so great.")

Inspiring Student Writers: Strategies and Examples for Teachers
pp. 145–157

My mother lost her fake smile, turned her head to the right ever so slightly, turned back to make eye contact with her daughter, and said in a mix of imploration and information: "But you're Jewish. *We're* Jewish."

"I know," my sister replied, and went back to eating dinner.

My mother looked blankly at my father who sat opposite her at the other end of the table. Dad was behind me. I don't know how he reacted, because I didn't look. I pretended to be absorbed in my meal.

After that ... nothing happened. But I'm sure we had ice cream for dessert. (In other words, "business as usual.") There was no follow-up or family meeting, and I've never discussed this with any members of my family, even though we talk and laugh about all kinds of things—*especially* those awkward, ohmygawwwwd! family moments. This was clearly one of them, but it has never come up.

But I knew my Mom was horrified. And sad. And hurt. And bewildered. I could see it. Dad must have felt the same.

It was clear my parents didn't want to pursue the matter. This was a perfect time for a lecture, and my parents were bright, articulate individuals who were involved in their Reform (i.e., liberal) Jewish community. They could have brought out all kinds of powerful examples and lobbied for Jewish pride. But they didn't. At the time, and for years thereafter, I imagined them devastated—poleaxed by those four words from one of their offspring. I don't know whether they followed up later, privately, with my sister, although I'm pretty certain my mom did.

I sat silently, not sharing my mom's upset, because I knew *exactly* what my sister meant. Part of me wanted to help her out, but at age 11, I was too savvy. I could have tried to explain her point, but I knew this was no mere intellectual discussion, no simple debate in which to engage my parents. The bomb had been dropped. Invisible shrapnel shards had found their mark. And as intelligent as my parents were, I didn't believe they—as Will Smith would rap about decades later—had the ability to understand. I knew there was a thick layer of emotion between my parents and the point my sister was making, and—to use a contemporary expression—I was not about to "go there."

PLEASE ... LET ME EXPLAIN

For the record: I like Jews. As the old expression goes, some of my best friends are Jews. In fact, I love a lot of them. But there are some Jews I don't like, and over the years, there have been quite a number of them.

What exactly did my sister mean? Exploring her statement beyond its literal level is important, not in terms of understanding Jews, *but in regard to understanding people*. Her statement in its broadest sense is not unique to our family or our culture. It has universal implications. There really are some people "whom only a mother could love."

The famed developmental psychologist, Jean Piaget (1896-1980), theorized that human beings spend their lives motivated to make sense of the world by gathering and arranging information (Piaget, 1954, 1963). We are "wired" to do this—genetically predisposed to this endeavor. Think of the brain as a massive computer hard drive comprised of a plethora of directories and files: food, shelter, transportation, fashion, people, politics, recreation, religion, travel, leisure, emotions, and so on. Take food. Imagine *all* the files and subfiles (pun intended). Consider all the files on people—including cross-categorical references based on personality, religion, race, and ethnicity.

We establish these files ("schemes" as Piaget dubbed them) at the start of life, at the commencing of thought, and we add to and modify them throughout our lives. Sometimes information comes pouring in. Other times it trickles in. Sometimes files are bursting with information. Sometimes they are almost barren.

When you understand this, you begin to realize how we, as humans, have the tendency to stereotype. As we seek to understand, a file with little information makes us prone to generalize, to make extreme leaps, sometimes logical and, at others, illogical—often in inaccurate and misleading ways.

Here's a favorite example. My son's pediatrician, Dr. R.M. Christian, had a wonderful bedside manner, equipped with a warm smile and the ability to make a patient feel cared for and loved. Dr. Christian also happened to be bald. He had such an impact on my son that when Daniel heard the question "What would you like to be when you grow up?", he inevitably replied: "A doctor ... a doctor like Dr. Christian." However, one day, after responding to the question, 4-year-old Daniel asked: "Does that mean I'll have to shave my hair off?"

Theoretically, a scheme filled with information guards against stereotypical leanings. But how much information is necessary to avoid oversimplified thinking? For my sister and me, no strangers to Jewish people and culture, we'd stored up LOTS of information. We had been surrounded by Jewish people and custom all our lives—our family, relatives, neighbors and their children, friends, fellow students, people at the synagogue, local merchants. We'd been adding to and adjusting this scheme for a long time—*years*. It's only natural then, in our continual quest to make sense of the world, that we would develop opinions about Jewish people—as well as many, many other things.

For example, during my pre-teen years, I knew I didn't like Japanese people. As opposed to my scheme on Jews, my Japanese scheme was extremely limited. But that didn't stop me from forming a very decided opinion. I don't remember ever pausing to remind myself: *You don't know ANY Japanese people; you've never even met any Japanese people.* I formed my opinion based on what I *did* know:

1. The Japanese were our enemy in WWII.
2. They had attacked Pearl Harbor.
3. When my friends and I played army, which we did a lot, we always fought the bad guys—the "Japs."
4. I had seen "Japs" in several war movies on TV, and judging from those characters, they were—clearly—a menacing, barbaric, scary group.

While there was not much in my scheme, there was enough to form a strong opinion, a strong stereotype. I had a similar scheme involving Native Americans, also composed without my knowing any Native Americans. It was based on watching a lot of Westerns in the 1950s and concluding that Indians (or "injuns") were—clearly—a menacing, barbaric, scary group. However, I was a big fan of *one* Indian—Tonto, the Lone Ranger's loyal sidekick. Tonto was a notable exception, but he spoke funny. He wasn't a savage, like *all* the other movie Indians I saw, but he also wasn't "on the same level" as the Lone Ranger.

It is embarrassing and painful to dredge up those old thoughts. But, and this is important to note, in both cases I was not aware that I was stereotyping. I didn't know that concept. I had no idea I was doing something so potentially damaging, so unsophisticated, so wrong.

In an autobiographical account written in 2005, Clyde Edgerton, best known as a writer of fiction, looked back on his perception of Native Americans while growing up in the 1950s and 1960s:

> If an American Indian had interviewed me when I was eighteen, would I have been able to explain the fact that so much of my boyhood—playtime, reading time, movie-viewing time—was spent killing pretend Indians or reading about their being killed or seeing them killed because they were all *bad*, and not worth much? And my enjoyment in killing pretend Indians was not because they were a threat—we'd already killed god knows how many of them over a couple of hundred years. Part of my enjoyment came from the fact that I had a young, impressionable human heart in my time (the 1950s and 1960s) and place (an America where non-Caucasians were often considered inferior and were advertised as such). (Edgerton 2005, p. 272)

DISEQUILIBRIUM—THE GUARD AGAINST STEREOTYPES

Piaget's theory of cognitive development explains that life is more complicated than merely setting up categories and filling them with information. After we create a scheme, we begin slipping in new bits of knowledge ("assimilation"). But sometimes we need to alter a scheme. For example, imagine a child at the zoo looking at a large lion. He overhears an adult say, "That is one big cat." The child has both a cat and a lion scheme, and he finds it humorous that a grown-up doesn't know the difference. He tells this to his parent, who says, "Actually, the lion is a member of the cat family."

Sometimes we can't simply tweak a scheme; we need to develop a new one. Piaget labels these adjustment processes as "accommodation." For instance, picture a child out in the woods who tells his parent he wants to "pet the funny looking cat over there—the black one with the white stripe down its back." He wants to assimilate this "cat" into his scheme, but in an instant, he's gathered up and whisked off to safety. Once secure, he learns this is not a matter of adding to his cat scheme. He's got to construct a brand new scheme: skunks.

Once people think stereotypically, it can be hard to change. Some develop stereotypes early in life and carry them to the grave. However, sometimes—inevitably—we are forced to question a scheme. We confront an exception. Piaget describes this state as "disequilibrium"—a condition that may leave us bothered, confused, angered, perplexed, uncomfortable. One response is to *ignore* the exception. In this case the stereotype remains.

But in our drive to make sense of the world, ignoring sometimes fails as an option. As much as we'd like to ignore, we must confront. In a state of disequilibrium, we seek to restore balance—both emotional and intellectual. Today's educational psychology texts refer to this as "a complex balancing act," and Piaget felt we are continually involved in this process.

Disequilibrium is a safeguard against stereotyping. Sometimes moving from that troubled state to equilibration (back to balance, understanding, awareness) is quick and easy. Sometimes it is lengthy ... *extremely* lengthy, even to the point of lasting a lifetime. Consider the example of a 4-year-old Caucasian child, Reggie, who is exposed *everyday* to a father who complains about Hispanics. "Those Hispanics are nothing but dirty, lazy bums," says the dad constantly. As a result, the child creates a Hispanic scheme. He can't help it. This is not something he can choose to avoid. In it are four bits of information: (1) Hispanics are people. (2) They are dirty. (3) They are lazy. (4) They are bums. The fact that Reggie has no idea what a Hispanic person actually looks and sounds like does not stop him from forming this scheme.

Let's continue this illustration. Reggie goes to a daycare, and one day a new child enters the program. He and Reggie become immediate best buddies. There is an instant bond; the two are inseparable—sharing a chemistry of friendship and humor and connection bolstered by a love of climbing, drawing, dinosaurs, and playing with blocks. Reggie gets to meet his new friend's parents, and he likes them immediately.

One day the daycare teacher launches into a lesson on diversity. "You are a wonderful group of children," she says, "and while you have a lot in common like your ability to learn and grow, your ability to be friendly and helpful, there are also differences you all have." She leads the children into a discussion of those differences: Some are boys; some are girls. Some are taller than others. Some have different likes and dislikes. "We also may look different based on certain physical features, like the color and texture of our hair and the color of our skin," she says. "That's because we come from different races. For example, in our group we have children who are White and Black and Hispanic."

Hispanic!? thinks Reggie, bewildered. *Hispanic kids … here?!*

And when the teacher asks the Hispanic children to stand, Reggie's best friend pops up.

Welcome to disequilibrium, Reg. He has got to confront his Hispanic scheme. The good news: He has some very powerful, very positive, first-hand information to move into his file. This authentic learning should force Reggie to face the stereotype, see its flaws, and broaden his consciousness. That's not the way 4-year-old Reggie will "see" this, but he is certainly capable of doing those things.

However, there is another scheme Reggie must confront—his dad scheme. As to finding harmony with our parental schemes, I know a lot of folks who spend their entire lives trying to find balance with these schemes … and not necessarily succeeding.

BACK TO MY SISTER AND ME

When we were growing up, we lived in an affluent suburb of Boston among mostly Jews and a few gentiles. My parents belonged to a Jewish country club, and while they played golf, the children played in and about the pool. This environment was filled with Jews; they came in all shapes and sizes, all ages, and they were quite well off monetarily (i.e., rich). In the club *milieu* was a non-Jewish minority—a fairly non-vocal, nonpowerful, hard working, mostly pleasant, inconspicuous group whose roles were relegated to caddying, cleaning, cooking, gardening, and so forth.

Jewish people populated our world. Plenty of them we liked. Many we loved. So what prompted my sister to make her Sunday lunch declaration, and what made me so understanding? First, our ages and levels of sophistication (or the lack thereof) are important factors. But let me analyze her statement in terms of Piaget's principles.

Jewish adults were not merely lumped into our "adult" scheme. Jewish adults were ensconced in their own, special scheme—a scheme much fuller, much more developed than our knowledge of "other adults." While some were extremely nice and friendly and warm, other were—in varying degrees—arrogant, pushy, inconsiderate, defensive, rude, opinionated, short-tempered, aloof, mean-spirited, backbiting, and hypocritical. Many of them said a lot of exaggerated, nasty things about people who weren't Jews—like Christians ("*goyim*") and Black people. As a child I knew this kind of behavior was wrong. I hadn't yet learned the word "racist."

My sister and I were also exposed to adults who were not Jews, and while many clearly could have been described with those aforementioned negative characteristics, they did not dwell in such a *concentrated, contained* environment. The country club was a ghetto—albeit a lavish, well appointed one, a "safe" place where the seeds of xenophobia, ethnocentrism, and racism could—and did—sprout. (These characteristics are true of many clubs, aren't they?)

And so, while I liked and loved many Jews, I also didn't like or love many Jews. That was my sister's point. And I understood why *many* other people (like some of the kids with whom I went to school) said they didn't like Jews. I mean, who does like arrogant, pushy, inconsiderate, defensive, rude, opinionated, short-tempered, aloof, mean-spirited, backbiting, and hypocritical people?

Another part of me understood, however, that when my parents heard my sister's words, they were processing things quite differently. And on that Sunday afternoon, I was ignoring—for the moment—my own continual disequilibrium that not only did many people not like Jews, they wanted to hurt and/or exterminate Jews. I had read and studied the Bible—Old and New Testament. Although I was young, my parents and others had educated me about the Nazi concentration camps, the 1950s blacklisting, the founding of Israel, and Jewish conspiracy mythology. There was plenty of stuff keeping me off balance.

And here's something else: I was a member of the Baby Boom generation. Other than a few name-calling incidents and "kike" references, I didn't experience any kind of sustained, problematic, disturbing prejudice from being Jewish, so as a pre-teenager, I didn't understand why these Jewish adults acted the way they did and exhibited—supposedly privately, among their own—such strong emotions. For me, being an upper-middle class Jew was a pretty sweet life, and I couldn't fully understand their rage, their suspicions. I wasn't aware of my privilege—not in a way that helped me empathize with others, especially those who had "paid their dues" and suffered to create the wonderful world I blithely strolled into.

THE BIGGER PICTURE

This is not an article about Jews. I'm talking about an experience, a perspective, a point of view shared by *billions and billions and billions* that spans races and ethnicities and religions.

Years ago, I listened to a woman at a party tell the following story about her 5-year-old son:

> So he comes home after the first day of kindergarten, and I greet him with a big smile and say, "How was your day?" And he says, "Good. Sorta good. All except for the Black kids. The Black kids are really mean. I don't like the Black kids." And I take him by the hand and walk him over to a mirror, and I say, "Look in the mirror, Brian. *You're* Black."

Is history not full of similar stories—not *bursting* with them?

I've heard people say terrible things about Jewish people—much of it stupid, illogical, stereotypical, and even laughably absurd. But the harshest, most constructive critics of Jews have been Jews.

I've heard people say terrible things about Black people—much of it stupid, illogical, stereotypical, and even laughably absurd. I've been a White teacher at a predominately Black university since 1978. The harshest, most constructive critics of Black people have been Black people. For instance, here is an example from my school's student newspaper, the *Campus Echo*. This column was written in September 2005 by Trésaun C. Lee, an African American woman:

More Than Skindeep

> I am exhausted in the classroom. I'm tired of my peers acting so immature and professors always relating everything we learn to being African-American. I feel so isolated from the rest of society, knowing that I spend the better part of my day discussing how it feels to be Black.
>
> I do understand that we attend an HBCU [historically Black college/university], and that its intention is to educate us about African-American history, but it is 2005 and I still feel oppressed. And not by white America or Bush, but by Black people.
>
> I have never seen such prejudice and self-hatred since I enrolled here. It's as if we despise each other for being so similar that we must scoff at our differences. It saddens me to witness a community of young Black students who cannot find the motivation to participate in class and are satisfied with a "C" because "at least it's not failing."
>
> Not only as students do we procrastinate, but as a race we are ultimately unsatisfied with ourselves. We are not pleased with our accomplishments unless we are rewarded. How many of us would give blood if we did not receive community service hours? Who are we to get upset when society calls

us lazy and says we don't reach for prominence? Who are we to want things when we do not give them?

We practically need that reassuring nod from our peers to know we are "accepted," but when their backs are turned, things change—smiles become snickers, and hospitality becomes ridicule—this recognition becomes null and void.

What others say doesn't often affect me, but I had the notion that I would be easily accepted at a Black university. But after being here for a year, I have noticed it is not just skin color that makes you Black. If you don't represent where you're from, then you are not Black. If you don't eat fried chicken with hot sauce, then you're not Black. If you don't listen to hip-hop or rap, then you're not Black. We are so wrapped up in being exploited that we don't realize we are demoralizing ourselves.

But being down here, I get the vibe that it's OK to be this way. In other words, disliking "uppity negroes" is the norm. This is not high school. I came here to get an education that will prepare me for a career, but a lot of students think this is just another four years to mess around. And too many professors condone it. They do not motivate us to participate or excite us about class.

Would any of this be happening if I didn't attend an HBCU? Honestly, I don't think it would; it seems we have this pre-set agenda for all Black people. Is it that our motivation only goes as far as it gets us personal gain? I believe it's NCCU's job to teach us to be citizens with pride in our education and then and only then will being Black be just my skin color, not my place in society.

We adjust our schemes throughout our lives. The process is ongoing. As a Jew, I understand there is a lot about being Jewish I don't understand and may never understand. Therefore, it's only logical that I will have the same problems of awareness and understanding with other groups—Muslims, Hispanics, Blacks, Asians, and so on.

Here are three things I rarely think about happening to me:

1.   being racially profiled;
2.   being followed around in a store—a suspected shoplifter; and
3.   fearing the police.

When I was younger, I had no idea what a burden, what an ordeal those omnipresent thoughts must be for certain people. Now that I'm older, now that I've studied the power of expectations, I respect (and am saddened by) the psychological weights others have to carry around ... constantly.

I was pulled over one time by a policeman. I knew I'd done nothing wrong, so I was very calm. But that changed when I saw him—hand on his revolver—approach my car. I was scared, even though I knew I'd done nothing wrong. And sure enough, it was a mistake. I was driving a car similar to one involved in a crime. "No problem," said the officer, smiling. And that's how I felt: no problem. The whole episode probably took no more than five minutes, but I still remember what that fear felt like, and how the feeling seemed to go on and on and on. I still remember that event from time to time. I doubt I'll experience a similar situation again.

But it's different for most of my students—especially my Black male students. Almost all of them—the vast majority—have had run-ins with the police. And the police don't smile. And when it's a mistake, the detaining sometimes goes on for hours—not minutes. And when it's a mistake, the guns are drawn. And sometimes, even if it's a mistake, even if my students are cooperating, they get pushed around and handcuffed ... or worse. And it doesn't happen once. Or twice. Or ... And unlike me, they can't simply relax and think: This probably will never happen again. Instead, they are *always* thinking about it happening, because it *does* happen again ... even though they have done nothing wrong.

My police "scheme" started early in my life. I still remember a friendly, perpetually smiling traffic cop who worked near my school. I remember teachers telling us that "policemen are our friends." I believed that instantly. And, for me, it has basically remained true my whole life. I expect it to remain so for the rest of my life. And I realize that probably the single defining characteristic of this probability is my white skin. And as I sit here and reflect on that last sentence, I think: *What a sad statement that is.* It makes me sad for people of color, but I am also saddened for policemen, because I understand that despite what may seem to be a simple situation, it is far from simple. It is a complicated, frustrating, maddening, frightening mess of psychology and sociology and xenophobia and ethnocentrism and racism.

WHO GETS TO DEFINE WHO WE ARE?

I consider myself a Jew, although I don't attend organized religious services and don't practice Judaism on an observable, formal basis. I have a sister who is a practicing conservative Jew. She doesn't consider me Jewish. Some might describe me as a "a lox and bagel Jew." That's a put-down, although it doesn't bother me. I know who I am, and this is a debate in which I'm not involved. I feel no need to defend my faith to others. Some people want to draw the lines, define the parameters, create the walls. Very Piaget-ish. Fine. I don't want to, because I don't see it the same way.

It makes me consider how different people define "Blackness" —particularly my Black students. Over the years I've heard them talk about Blackness as both a good and bad thing. Bad: "They were acting like a bunch of Black people." Good: "The blacker the berry, the sweeter the juice"—a folk saying used by Wallace Thurman for the title of his 1929 novel, *The Blacker the Berry*. A little while ago, there was a saying that could be interpreted as good or bad, depending on the situation: "It's a Black thing. You wouldn't understand."

Over the years, I've heard a number of Black students receive the staggering criticism from certain peers that they weren't Black enough. In many cases to underscore the point, these young men and women were routinely called "White boy" or "White girl." What caused this ethnic/racial transformation? Sometimes it had to do with dress. Sometimes it had to do with their refusal to use certain slang. Most often it related to excelling in school—being a dependable student, participating in class, speaking in standard dialect. Of course these taunts start well before the university level, and the phenomenon has been addressed by a number of researchers (e.g., Cross, 1995; Ogbu, 1999; Spencer, Noll, Stoltzfus, & Harpalani, 2001).

However, the research finds a different perspective within the Asian American community (Okagaki & Frensch, 1998; Portes, 1999). And yet, the stereotype of the "ideal" Asian American child is dismantled by Stacey J. Lee's interviews with Asian American teens who did *not* fit the positive stereotype in her powerful, haunting book—*Unraveling the "Model Minority" Stereotype: Listening to Asian American Youth* (1996). One point that emerged was the dubiousness of the term "good stereotype." As Lee's book offers valuable, often troubling insights by and about Asian American youth and their fight against or their willingness to embrace the "model minority" label, the reader may feel simultaneously frustrated and enlightened.

I think about my parents listening to my sister's comment, and I am reminded of Lee's dilemma when she confronted Korean adolescents *repulsed* at being labeled Asian American, viewing themselves as drastically different and obviously superior to other Asians. As one Korean teenager states: "I just don't like them [Asians who are not Korean] at all. I find them hideous. I wouldn't want to talk to them" (Lee, 1996, p. 19). Lee, a Chinese American, explains her reaction: "I was on the verge of blowing my ethnographer's poise and expressing my outrage. With some effort, I managed to maintain my composure" (Lee, 1996, p. 18). The book is brimming with complex emotional episodes and disclosures, and Lee's interviews with teenagers, teachers, and administrators often reveal a Lewis Carroll absurdity and a slough of simplistic, stereotypical beliefs.

INDIVIDUALS ... AND IRONY

Many claim that the answer to stereotyping is recognizing people as individuals. But it is the characteristics and actions of individuals that compose, fuel, and retrench stereotypes. There is no simple solution.

However, as befits the best stereotype debunkers, Lee's book introduces us to individuals. She breaks down Asian American adolescents into four distinct groups and acquaints us with students who reveal their motivations, fears, concerns, frustrations, and prejudices. The truth is often uncomfortable, disheartening. For example, one student, an Asian "new waver," rebels against the stereotype of Asian men as meek and sees his road to success in America via bulking up rather than buckling down; thus, he purposely flies in the face of several stereotypes. Is this good or not so good? Is that young man (a) a rebel, (b) a rebel without a cause, (c) a rebel without a clue, or (d) all of the above?

Lee does an excellent job of confronting the *supposed* "good stereotype"—explaining its tendency to lump all Asians together, to impose an expectation of passive behavior, and to pit other minority cultures and their stereotypes (often negative) against each other, while deflecting attention away from White racism. One student, in explaining Asian diversity, says, "If you don't do that well in math or science, the teacher is like, 'What are you? Some kind of mutant Asian?' ... a lot of my friends become upset if they're not good students ... I don't think it's right for them to have to feel defensive. And for people who are doing well, it's just like, 'Oh, they [Asians] didn't have to work for it.'" (Lee, 1996, p. 67)

For decades I've heard people use the term "the Black community," conjuring up this huge, yet simple, homogenous entity—this monolithic "thing" that, basically, thinks and acts the same way. And I've heard people, often intelligent people, say—and say quite often: "So what does the Black community feel about ...?" And they await an answer—as though there is *actually* an answer to this utterly stupid question. Because it *is* a stupid question.

As Piaget reminds us, we perform these kinds of cognitive operations—thinking in terms of the Hispanic community, White society, the elderly, Generation X, the poor, and so forth—because we *have* to; it's part of the arranging, the sorting, the trying to make sense. Stereotypes appeal to us, *even when we know they're wrong*, because they *simplify* life. People long for this all the time: "I've got to find a way to simplify my life." Who talks about making life more complicated?

A FINAL THOUGHT

Nowadays a common warning is "don't go there." For educators of multiculturalism, however, the process is all about "going there." The quest to attain the loftiest goals of multiculturalism—appreciation of and respect for diverse cultures—starts with knowledge, with awareness—filling those schemes with truths and plenty of 'em. In addition to supplying those facts and concepts and experiences, perhaps our greatest contribution as educators and parents and friends is to be disequilibrium catalysts.

The humanity that unites us, that makes us vulnerable to oversimplification, generalization, and stereotyping—understanding that can often be confusing, disturbing, embarrassing, even frightening. But confusion, disturbance, and fright are the triggers for disequilibrium, an imbalance between what we understand and what we confront. In some cases, we can chose to ignore, but it is hard—sometimes impossible—to ignore the truth. And that's a great virtue of disequilibrium—offering us opportunities to improve, to develop, to grow.

REFERENCES

Cross, W. E. (1995). Oppositional identity and African American youth: Issues and prospects. In W. D. Hawley & A. W. Jackson (Eds.), *Toward a common destiny: Improving race and ethnic relations in America* (pp. 185-204). San Francisco: Jossey-Bass.

Edgerton, C. (2005). *Solo: My adventures in the air.* Chapel Hill, NC: Algonquin Books of Chapel Hill.

Lee, S. J. (1996). *Unraveling the "model minority" stereotype: Listening to Asian American Youth.* new York: Teachers College Press.

Lee, T. C. (2005, September 28). More than skindeep. *Campus Echo* (the student newspaper at North Carolina Central University, Durham, NC), p. 12.

Ogbu, J. (1999, April). *The significance of minority status.* Paper present at the annual meeting of the American Educational Research Association, Montreal.

Okagaki, L., & Frensch, P. A. (1998). Parenting and children's school achievement: A multiethnic perspective. *American Educational Research Journal, 35*(1), 123-144.

Piaget, J. (1954). *The construction of reality in the child* (M. Cook, Trans.). New York: Basic Books.

Piaget, J. (1963). *Origins of intelligence in children.* New York: Norton.

Portes, P. R. (1999). Social and psychological factors in the academic achievement of children of immigrants: A cultural history puzzle. *American Educational Research Journal, 36*(3), 489-507.

Spencer, M. B., Noll, E., Stoltzfus, J., & Harpalani, V. (2001). Identity and school adjustment: Revisiting the "acting White" assumption. *Educational Psychologist, 36*(1), 21-30.

CHAPTER 18

HELPING STUDENT WRITERS UNDERSTAND AND DEAL WITH REJECTION

Tom Scheft

It's not easy for many us to accept criticism, even when it is absolutely justified. We appear to live in an age in which our defenses are perpetually up, and many of us tend to overvalue our abilities. Thousands and thousands of people audition hoping to become stars, convinced that their singing ability will launch them as the next Mariah or Sting—their narcissistic naiveté and delusional self-esteem gone wild, fueled over the years by fawning, terribly misguided "friends," parents, and relatives.

What happens when we criticize students' written work? How open are they to being told their ideas, points, examples are confused, awkward, dull, vague, clichéd, simplistic, boring, unrealistic? (Rhetorical question.) Nobody wants to hear that, *especially* when it's true.

I don't have an answer for this. (If I did, I'd be writing this from my estate in Hawaii.)

We need to teach students about the value of criticism. We need to teach them *how* to criticize effectively. We need to show them that criticism—thoughtful, helpful feedback—is part of the writing process, with the purpose of improving their work.

Inspiring Student Writers: Strategies and Examples for Teachers
pp. 159–175
Copyright © 2009 by Information Age Publishing
159

One popular strategy is for *the teacher* to step up as pedagogical guinea pig/whipping boy, to subject his/her work for analysis and examination. These papers are instructional tools, with both strengths and weaknesses, compositions that offer students the opportunity to find fault and offer recommendations. The teacher's job is to model how to handle the criticism—agreeing, disagreeing, quibbling, standing firm, asking for specific solutions. This revising activity is based on a popular saying attributed to St. Jerome: "Good, better, best. Never let it rest. 'Til your good is better and your better is best."

While teachers typically role-play appropriate behavior, for the bold educator, one tactic is becoming the *bad* role model:

> Teacher: "What do you mean you don't like my introduction?! You're stupid. (pause) Okay, class, what problem did you just notice?"

Many students enjoy seeing teachers purposely demonstrate inappropriate behavior. It's disarming. We live in mean-spirited times. We want to make sure students know put-downs and teasing are not permissible and are counter-productive in certain situations.

Another popular technique: Before students begin critiquing each other, *have the class create a set of rules*—examples of what to say and what not to say, what to do and what not to do. Some possibilities:

1. Use "indoor voices" (AKA "six-inch voices," a quiet voice because the person is so close) and speak respectfully.
2. If you feel your criticism may come across as too harsh, get a second opinion from the teacher.

Another common practice is the use of a rubric or grading sheet:

Paper written by _____

Paper read by _____

1. Read the whole paper without stopping. Put a check in the left margin next to any line that was not clear or that you had to read twice. Note any appropriate concerns or errors like spelling, punctuation, or usage.

2. In no more than two sentences, explain the main point of the paper.

   _____
   _____

   _____

3. Rate the following:

		Great	Good	Okay	Poor
a.	Interesting beginning				
b.	Effective beginning				
c.	Clear thesis/main idea(s)				
d.	Specific examples				
e.	Sentence variety				
f.	Effective conclusion				
g.	Overall structure				
h.	Spelling				
i.	Usage				
j.	Punctuation				

4. The paper's length was ___ too short ___ too long ___ just right.

5. Does the paper show originality or creativity? If so, illustrate.

_____

_____

6. What is the best thing about this paper?

_____

_____

7. How might the paper be improved?

_____

_____

8. Other comments

_____

_____

Of course before you let the kids loose with this sheet, you've got to *teach it* to the class. You've got to model reading a paper, marking it, and filling out the form. Get your metacognitive juices flowing, teachers. Demonstrate your thoughts *out loud*.

You may need to do this activity a few times. Then, for homework, give everyone a sample paper to mark up. Next class, fill out one of the sheets as a guided practice. Note the different perspectives among the students. Allow people to explain their ratings. Make it clear: We don't always agree, *and we don't have to agree*. But we do need to be able to explain our reasoning thoughtfully and clearly. (And you may need to do *this* exercise several times before you feel the class is ready to pair up or share papers in small groups.)

Throughout the year from time to time, highlight great student examples. (This doesn't have to take a lot of time.) Bring in some not-so-stellar work (no names, please, no material by current students) and ask for remedies. Feature the work of professional writers. Create your own examples. (Here, let me give you a prompt: *It was the best of times. It was the …*)

No matter how proactive you are, no matter how cautious you try to be, somebody's feelings are going to get hurt. It's going to happen, and I don't have an answer to prevent it. (If I did, I'd be writing this from my castle in Switzerland.)

Rejection hurts, and writing is full of rejection—maddening, humiliating, embarrassing rejection. And when you do feel bad, ask yourself: *Is this as bad as the green bean story?*

Ah yes, the green bean story. Years ago, one of my graduate students told the class that whenever her kids got upset, she would ask them: "Is this as bad as the green bean story?"

The Green Bean Story: A True Story

Once upon a time, a young woman was on her way to Virginia to meet her boyfriend's parents for the first time. A 20-year-old, she was quite nervous, because while she came from a lower-middle class family, her boyfriend's parents were, as they say, "stinkin' filthy rich." Added to that, she was late to dinner.

As she drove into the majestic grounds of the lavish estate, she found it hard to breathe. Everything was so beautiful. There in the distance stood the mansion. As she neared the front door, the house loomed larger and larger.

She parked the car and rushed inside. There seated in an enormous dining room were the family, her boyfriend, and various guests. Servants soundlessly whisked away plates, brought new delicacies, and kept glasses filled to the brim. Her boyfriend motioned her to sit beside him, and then proceeded to introduce her to the group. Beaming, but even more daunted by the opulence, she quickly sat, picked up a fork and began to partake of the dinner—starting with a green bean, which she cut in two, speared, then deposited in her mouth.

At that point, suddenly short of breath, she began to cough—first a bit quietly, then louder and louder, until all conversation ceased, and all eyes were upon her. As she attempted to swallow the bean, a final, flagrant cough emerged—sending the bean up into her nasal cavity … and out her right nostril—a vibrant, half-inch green cylinder.

So when you're feeling rejected, ask yourself: *Is this as bad as the green bean story?*

IT HAPPENS TO THE PROS

Jennifer Minah (2003), a freelance writer and the managing editor of *Writer's Break*, notes the inescapable rejection writers face in her Web-based article, "Understanding Rejection Slips":

All writers suffer rejection. Yes, even the greats. An editor from the *San Francisco Examiner* sent this in a rejection letter to Rudyard Kipling: "I am sorry, Mr. Kipling, but you just do not know how to use the English language." Even e.e. cummings wasn't immune to rejection. Did you know it was cummings' mother who first published his poems after a dozen publishers rejected them? Beatrix Potter's *The Tale of Peter Rabbit* was rejected at least six times before she published it herself. If these acclaimed authors faced rejection, why wouldn't you or I?

And if those names aren't big enough, how about Harry Potter author J. K. Rowling? What about Alex Haley, author of *Roots*? Most successful writers are those who hung in there.

As James Scott Bell (2004) notes in his Web article, "Rejecting Rejection," "it's comforting to know that rejection happens to all writers, no matter how well known." He talks of William Saroyan, one of his "writing heroes … [who] collected a pile of rejection slips thirty inches high—some seven thousand—before he sold his first short story!" When Bell pursued a writing career and endured a "period of constant rejection," he sought support from "[one of] my favorite little books, *Rotten Rejections*" (Pushcart Press), which chronicles the obstacles faced by famed writers. He mentions Zane Grey, a best-selling author, who early in his career received this feedback from an editor: "I do not see anything in this [novel] to convince me you can write either narrative or fiction." Bell also notes that George Orwell received the following advice on his classic *Animal Farm*: "It is impossible to sell animal stories in the U.S.A."

A LITTLE CLOSER TO HOME

My brother Bill is, according to many people, a comic genius. He's been a stand-up comic, a writer for a number of comedy shows and roasts, and a writer for "Late Night with David Letterman" and "The Late Show With David Letterman" for over 16 years. He is also a wonderful novelist, having publishing *The Ringer* and *Time Won't Let Me*, a Thurber Award finalist.

Maybe I'm not the most objective guy around (Did I mention he's my *brother*, the comic genius?), but Bill has a unique ability to blend comedy and wit into literature. And when I say "unique," I'm not just throwing out a compliment. He has a singular voice as an author and an ability to manipulate contrasting tones—blurring the line between comedy and pathos, reality and fiction. Here are some favorite examples:

Richie Lyman, John Thiel, Tim Schlesinger, and Jerry Fyne were hardly friends. They had fought on opposite sides during the Fire Extinguisher

Wars for their respective dorms, Mulvihill (Richie and John) and Grays (Tim and Jerry). Richie and Jerry had shared one intimate prep school moment the previous spring as freshmen when half a dozen juniors dunked their heads in an unflushed toilet for the unpardonable sin of being Jewish.

Tim Schlesinger had been excused from the Freshman Yid Roundup. Medical reasons. The post-knee-surgery cast on his leg made it impossible to kneel commodeward. It was his second operation since football, when a bad foot plant on worse turf ripped his knee in two directions and his four-year, three-sport career was finished, a destination he had never anticipated. By February, he was begging his parents to humanely yank him out of Chase [Academy] and let him hobble at North High, where he would be merely a guy on crutches rather than the Jew cripple. (*Time Won't Let Me*, p. 2)

*   *   *

Thanks to a shrink with a heart in triplicate, Mort took enough Valium to make absolutely no difference if he took two more. So much, he used the Latin neuter plural when describing his dosage. It was not fifty milligrams of Valium a day. It was "five *valia*." Five blue valia. Check. Five periwinkle valia. Or ten canary valia. The *valia* wordplay was one of those rare occasions when Mort would entertain himself. It was the third generation of a joke Alistair Cooke told him one night at P.J. Moriarty's. Julius Caesar walks into a bar. Tells the bartender, "I'll have a martinus." Bartender says, "Don't you mean a martini?" And Caesar says, "If I wanted a double, I'd ask for it!" A week later, Mort had Alistair banging the table and wiping his eyes with P.J. Moriarty's starchiest linen when he asked the waiter for a "vodkum" on the rocks. "Don't you mean vodka, Mr. Spell?" You already know the rest. And it only got funnier the next III or IV rounds. (*The Ringer*, p. 16-17)

*   *   *

There were things, other lines, that College Boy wanted to say all the time on the [softball] field. Funny stuff. But he couldn't. Every time some self-important actor in the Performing Arts or Show Business League went down on a called strike, College Boy was dying to yell, like some casting director, "Thank you!" But he couldn't. Or when a fat guy, any fat guy, came up and he was all set to cry out "Throw him a salad." But he couldn't. One time, the shortstop for *Cats* bobbled three ground balls in a row and College Boy was this close to saying, "It's *Cats*. He'll play with the ball for an hour, till he gets bored." But he didn't. He couldn't. College Boy was paid to do a lot of things on a softball field, and after hitting and fielding, number three on the list was *not* to ridicule the 95 percent who weren't being paid. (*The Ringer*, p. 50-51)

*   *   *

College Boy recognized the stance. Randy Zank.

Randy Zank was the best baseball player every coughed up by Lynn South High School. Before College Boy was College Boy, he was just another kid in Lynn trying to catch Randy Zank. He couldn't. He wouldn't try. In June 1969, Randy Zank graduated from Lynn South and headed for the Mekong Delta, where they had a shortage of mythic figures. Six months in, the littlest piece of cartilage had lost to an even littler piece of shrapnel. He returned to Lynn, where he was greeted by the normal indifference extolled upon a Vietnam vet, plus the bonus resentment of a town cheated out of a big league career. The limp from his 5 percent Teflon knee was now barely perceptible. (*The Ringer*, p. 151)

*   *   *

If your goal is to be left alone, nothing will turn the collective back of the public on you like Parkinson's Disease. A slight tremor, usually in the fingers or hands, is the opening metaphor for the rocking of your world. And like any good metaphor, it is sustained. The brochure will tell you Parkinson's is a neurological disorder that can strike anyone over thirty. In the world of diseases, it is a mystery. A bad mystery, with little plot, no hero, and an end that drags out long enough to hopelessly point fingers in every direction. Technically—and anybody knows people never use the word "technically" unless they want to back up a really weak point—technically, no one ever dies from Parkinson's Disease. But everyone is lost.

College Boy first noticed the tremors in Mort's hands three weeks after his uncle was released from Mount Sinai. They were out at a Japanese restaurant, and he saw that neither of them was using chopsticks. College Boy had an excuse, the casts [from his softball injury], but Mort was eating his sashimi by hand. Normally, Morton Martin Spell took great pride in his chopstick dexterity and never missed a chance to tease his nephew about how he grabbed his sticks too low. "You're choked up a little too much, kid," he'd say, "unless you're trying to hit that maguro to shallow right field." College Boy became aware of the shaking when Mort switched from vodka to tea. Until then, it just sounded like any concerned drinker trying help his ice along.

"What's with your hands, Mort?"

"They're idling." (*The Ringer*, p. 139)

Now Bill has his diehard fans and his admirers, but he also has his critics. And sometimes they say scathing things, like this example from *Publishers Weekly*:

There is rarely even a snicker is this supposedly comic first novel by a monologue writer for David Letterman.

[later in the review] [Certain] New York [minor characters] are well conceived, but even they can't keep Scheft's tale from falling flat.

Huh? What book were you reading and exactly how many bottles of cough syrup did you chug first?

And it's not just critics. Bill has had to deal with agents and editors who don't always get what's going on in his books. I'll let Bill give you an example:

> About ten years ago, I was the head writer for the ESPY Awards. I had written an opening piece for the host that year, actor Jimmy Smits, which he liked. A few days before we went on the air, an executive from ESPN whom I had never met before had a meeting with me and the producer to go over the script. The following is a reasonably exact transcript.
>
> ESPN executive: I've read the script, and I like it. The only problem I have is with the opening.
>
> Me: What is the problem?
>
> ESPN executive: Well, I don't get it.
>
> Me: Is that really a problem? That you don't get it? Because I get it, and the host of your show gets it. So, the fact that you don't get it really doesn't bother me. I'm okay with that.
>
> Here's my point: Don't do that, even if you can get away with it. But here's my other point: "I don't get it" is not a valid criticism. It is a disrespectful dismissal, and it is not about your work. One of your duties as a writer is to seek feedback. But your responsibility, as a writer seeking feedback, is that it sometimes requires you to actually, uh, seek the feedback. Which means you may need to ask simple questions. So, for every "I don't get it" (and get ready for a lot of that, especially if you choose a career writing for television), you need to ask, "Can you be more specific?" or "Is there something that is unclear?"
>
> Now, the responses you get may be, "No. It's just everything" or "Hmm. No. It's just everything." And while these are aggravating, they are illuminating. They tell you all you need to know about *the critiquer*. And you cannot take them seriously or personally. But you need to take your work seriously and personally. So, make the effort, ask the questions, and accept that the results of that effort are not up to you. In the meantime, feel free to live vicariously through that story.

And then there are folks who buy Bill's books—expecting them to be filled with Lettermanian *shtick*. And when they are confronted by something other than their expectations, some get upset or disappointed. And they're not content to keep their feelings to themselves, because we live in the age of the Internet, and *anybody* can be a critic. All you gotta do is start typing. Brain cells optional.

It's hard putting yourself out there as a writer. And I know the late Rick Nelson sang, "You see, you can't please everyone, so you got to please yourself," but come on. Even when the world is full of readers who love your work, for some writers, the criticism is never easily dealt with.

Writing books is "a bit less disposable an endeavor than writing for television," says Bill, and the comments you receive on your work reflect that, because the process is much longer and much more involved. It has to be. "A half-hour sitcom script is 45 pages and can be written in a weekend," he notes. "A novel is at least 300 pages and usually takes a couple of years before it's suitable for submission to a publisher—unless you're Stephen King and can dash one off waiting in line at the DMV."

THE ROLE OF AN EDITOR

"The editor-writer relationship can be intimate, intense, and occasionally contentious," says my brother, "especially at the beginning when the editor is trying to impart his vision for your work. Every editor wants to make every book better. His job at the publishing house depends on it." As Bill explains, in the beginning, "the notes and critiques will come fast, furious and frothy." But, warns Bill, "and these are the keys to the kingdom I am giving you: Most times, editors voice suggestions for changes in your work that they believe in passionately. Sometimes, they are just clearing their throats. Sadly, the passionate belief and the throat-clearing sound exactly the same. You need to differentiate."

Bill's first novel is about a 35-year-old hired gun softball player whose life changes when he has to take care of his ailing uncle. He met his editor for the first time at a hotel bar. I'll let Bill pick up the story:

> We sat down over drinks and he gave me three notes: First, he wanted to change the title from *Say Nephew* to *The Ringer*. Fine. Done. Second, he needed me to write two very short chapters up front to get the plot rolling quickly before I dealt in character studies. Fine. Done.
>
> My editor drained his second Absolut on the rocks and told me the third note: "And listen to me. If you want this book to be a classic, an absolute classic, you cannot have College Boy and the uncle leave New York and go to Boston. It is a huge mistake that they leave. They need to stay in New York. Once they leave, you lose all the dramatic tension."
>
> My editor then excused himself to go to the men's room, which lost all the dramatic tension at the table. I was glad for the break. I didn't agree with his last point. Not at all. When he returned, I said, "With all due respect, I'm not keeping everyone in New York. The second half of the book is in Boston because everyone is leaving their former lives behind."
>
> His response: "But it's *The Ringer*, and you'll do the two short chapters up front?"
>
> Me: "Oh yeah."
>
> His response: "Dynamite. Honey, can I get a refill?"

The story has a happy ending. *The Ringer* came out to wonderful reviews, except for *Publishers Weekly*, which I had completely forgotten about until now. *(Sniff.)* Give me a minute.

Let's analyze Bill's above story in terms of his earlier point: *Is there something that is unclear?*—which he says "is the key element in any valid criticism . . . and the writer's only capital offense." First, the novel's original title, *Say Nephew*, was a play on the expression "Say uncle." Clever, but the editor's change to *The Ringer* is terrific, especially in terms of marketing and providing a sharper focus for the buyer/reader. Second, the editor advised two, short beginning chapters to establish the story better. You can understand why Bill had no hesitation.

Says my brother, "Nobody will like everything you write. But if a section or character or plotline is unclear, that is on you. Somebody reads your piece and says, 'I don't like Lester.' It happens. But, if somebody reads your piece and says, 'I liked Lester, but he just disappeared after page 5,' and your reply is, 'Well, he died on page 4,' and their reply is, 'He died? Really? Lester? The plumber? I had no idea,' chances are Lester did not get a proper sendoff."

Here's another example. When Bill sold his second novel (about a prep school garage band that tries to reunite 30 years after the members learn the vanity album they made in 1967 is worth $10,000), he received the first pass of notes back from his editors:

There were six major points. Four I begrudgingly agreed with, easy enough fixes. But the other two I was horrified by. They could not believe an album made by five 18-year-olds no one ever heard of could be that valuable. It was as if they had completely missed the plot of the book and decided to write their own. There's only one thing worse than a guy saying, "I don't get it." A guy who thinks he got it and missed it completely. I was ready to chuck the whole thing. I sought the humane counsel of my older brother, who said, quite simply, "Maybe they need to be educated a little."

So, I called the editor who had bought the book and first told him about all the points I agreed with. (Remember: Stroke first. Writers aren't the only ones who want platitudes.) Then I carefully addressed his other concerns, explaining in detail how I had arrived at the storyline I had chosen. He told me to get it all down in an email and send it to him and the fiction editor.

Two days later, they got back to me. They said, "You need to explain the idiosyncrasies of record collecting and what makes an album this valuable," and "You need to show what made this prep school band, The Truants, so special. Let's see them onstage."

So, in two days, they had gone from thinking I needed to completely rework the plot to making me clarify two aspects of the book I had glanced over in my need to push characters along. Indeed, they needed to be educated a little. And I, in turn, needed to educate the reader. When all was said and done, it took about five pages, and made the book infinitely better.

Notes Bill, "The longer I write, the simpler the reason I write gets: Do good work, get better. Writers write, and every part of the process, including criticism and its occasionally elusive offspring, clarity, is essential. Got it?"

NEVER GIVING UP

Sure, we'd all like to join The Successful, Acclaimed Writers Club, but the membership is small; the initiation is extremely rough; and learning the secret handshake is a killer. The vast majority of us who take pen to paper or fingers to keyboard won't get an invitation.

Some people have that special something that sets them apart as artists. Many feel that way about the paintings of Vincent Van Gogh. But Vinnie, we're told, never sold any of his paintings during his lifetime, except for one that was purchased *by his brother* four months before his death.

Some people have that special something that sets them apart as writers. Even then, that's not enough to get a contract. John Kennedy Toole wrote a novel, but none of the publishing houses he sent it to wanted to buy it. Toole committed suicide. Eleven years later in 1980, after a campaign launched by Toole's mother and writer Walker Percy, Toole's book, *A Confederacy of Dunces*, was published, became a cult classic, and won the Pulitzer Prize for Fiction in 1981.

And if you manage to stay alive and get that chance to publish a novel, your dream may die quickly, as your books are unceremoniously dumped in the remainder bin and your career as a writer ends abruptly. Life is tough, says the bumper sticker, and then you die.

But we dream. Many of us dream of being published authors. When I talk to students of pursuing that dream, I tell them about my friend, Clyde Edgerton—an author known and respected nationally and internationally. Long before he became famous, Clyde—like many writer/dreamers—had the vision and the desire and the talent, but at one point, that was almost not enough.

Growing up, Clyde didn't think about being a writer. Like a lot children, he thought about being a professional baseball player or a pilot. His mother, Truma Warren Edgerton, had hopes her son would become a concert pianist or a missionary. Today, Clyde plays a mean keyboard. As for the missionary part, well ....

Clyde began writing fiction in December of 1977. A 33-year-old professor in the School of Education at Campbell University in Buies Creek,

North Carolina, he had discovered a soft spot in the kitchen floor of his Apex, North Carolina, home; then he found there was an old well under the floor, and condensation from the remaining water was weakening the flooring. These ingredients inspired his first short story about a boy falling through a kitchen floor into a well, which would later be included in his third novel, *The Floatplane Notebooks*.

I had known Clyde since 1972. He was, and still is, a funny, clever, insightful, thoughtful person—a lot of fun to be around. If anybody was going to emerge as a successful writer, placing your money on C.E. was a good bet.

In May 1978, Clyde viewed a PBS broadcast of author Eudora Welty reading her short story "Why I Live at the P.O." Watching the famed writer motivated Clyde "to write seriously." He began the next morning.

That summer, he wrote four short stories and started sending them out to various magazines and journals. He wrote a few more stories by February 1979, and he sent those out.

And then he began receiving rejection notices—dozens and dozens. As the number of negative letters rose higher and higher by late 1979, Clyde considered giving up writing fiction. Completely. For the first time in his life, he was forced to face a stream of constant rejection; it was an uncomfortable surprise and shock to an individual who had consistently known academic, athletic, and social success.

I remember the day. I'd just dropped by his home for a visit. Clyde and I have spent most of our friendship joking around, but on that day his face was very solemn when he came to the door. As we walked back to the kitchen, he said, "I don't think I'm going to be writing any more fiction."

"What do you mean?" I asked.

He stopped at a small table, reached down, and grabbed up a stack of opened mail. "All the letters," he said. "I'm tired of all the rejection."

I didn't say anything.

He put the letters down.

There was a pause, an awkward silence, and then—typical of two guys—we just dropped the subject. Who knows? Probably one of us punched the other in the arm. At the time, I was aware this was an important, heartfelt statement from my friend, and I was speechless. I knew he was serious. This was no idle threat, no begging for a compliment. I could feel all that, and perhaps that is why I didn't, *couldn't*, speak at that moment.

The very next day, however, on the verge of abandoning his dream of being a fiction writer, Clyde received a two-page, single-spaced letter from the editor of *Just Pulp*—a small, federally-funded literary magazine out of New Jersey. The editor had read that first short story and offered this basic review: interesting tale, needs work. He included his editing recommendations.

Rejuvenated, Clyde diligently revised and resubmitted the story. And the editor replied: It needs more work. He included additional recommendations.

Once again, Clyde revised and resubmitted.

Now, if you're thinking: *Okay, so the story was accepted*, you'd only be partially right. The editor's next letter was a stunning example of good news/bad news. The good news: We accept your story. The bad news: We have no money to publish the magazine.

Ah, but there was a happy ending. The funds finally came through, and the story, "Natural Suspension," was published. Clyde was paid a-quarter-of-a-cent per word, earning him a little over four dollars.

But he was more inspired than ever. He was a *published* fiction writer. There was no giving up now.

From 1979 to 1984, Clyde circulated 12 short stories. During that period, he received six acceptances (three by friends). He also received 202 rejections. 2—0—2.

One of his short stories, "Privacy," which was based on a true story, featured an ongoing conflict between a female—a product of the small town, white, middle class, ultraconservative South—and a male—a product of upper-middle class, liberal, big city Atlanta. Clyde had a vision of expanding it into a novel, using the female character, Raney, to tell the story of her turbulent, values-challenged relationship with fiancé Charles Shepherd.

It took 2 years to complete the novel *Raney*, which was then rejected by 11 agents and publishing houses.

However, Clyde—learning that Louis Rubin, an esteemed English professor at the University of North Carolina, was starting his own publishing house—sent him two chapters, a baseball book (knowing of Rubin's fondness for the game), and $10 to cover reading expenses.

A short time later, Rubin informed Edgerton he had ripped up check, liked the chapters, and urged Clyde to send a finished manuscript to his chief editor, Shannon Ravenel, at the newly founded Algonquin Books. Clyde wasted little time.

Ravenel liked the novel for the most part, but felt there were needed changes. Algonquin offered Clyde a first option contract for $250, agreeing to publish the book if the revision went well, but also having the first right of refusal.

Following Ravenel's suggestions, Clyde spent six months revising, and *Raney* was accepted in the fall of 1983 for $250. A spring 1985 publication date was set.

He had worked on the novel off and on from late 1979 to fall 1983, so the money didn't begin to cover all the blood, sweat and tears he'd exhausted, but for Clyde this first major publication was about much more than money. This was a special triumph and with it came a distinct joy, which undoubtedly helped him laugh off the banner headline in his local newspaper, *The Western Wake Herald* (Apex, NC):

Local Author Publishes
Novel After 202 Rejections

At this time in Algonquin's early history, the typical press run for a new book was 3,000 copies. At the last minute, Rubin decided to print 5,000 copies—figuring they might gather dust for a number of years, but eventually they'd sell.

All the books quickly sold out.

As a matter of fact, 10 printings of the hardback sold 20,000 copies very quickly, vastly ahead of expectations. *Raney* was the breakthrough novel for Algonquin Books, going on to sell 30,000 hardback copies and over 200,000 paperback copies. When people discuss the success of *Raney* and Clyde's other works, they often speak of his keen ear for dialect and dialogue, as well as his special gift for humor. I agree. For me, the novel contains the funniest piece of dialogue I've ever read (note the final line of this excerpt):

When Mrs. Register was out of hearing distance, Mama says, "Mr. Register just had a prostrate operation and I don't think he's recovered."

"Prostate," says Aunt Flossie.

"It is?" says Mama. "Prostate? Oh. You know, I've always liked him better than her. She always makes so much out of every little thing."

The conversation went from the Registers to prostrate operations back around to eating meat.

"You know," says Aunt Naomi, "once in a while I've gone without meat, but I got so weak I thought I'd pass out."

"Well, that happens a bit at first," Mrs. Shepherd says. "But after a few days that usually goes away. It's a matter of what you get used to, I think. The body adjusts."

"I'd be afraid I couldn't get enough proteins," says Mama.

"Oh, no," says Mrs. Shepherd. "There are many protein substitutes for meat. Beans—soybeans, for example—are excellent."

"My next door neighbor, Lillie Cox, brought me some hamburger with soybean in it," said Aunt Naomi, "when I had the flu last winter, and it tasted like cardboard. She's always trying out the latest thing."

"I couldn't do without my meat," says Mama. . . .

"I guess you have less cholesterol if you don't eat meat," says Aunt Naomi.

"There are health advantages," said Mrs. Shepherd. "And also our women's group has been concentrating on how eating less meat can help curtail hunger in the third world."

"On another *planet?*" says Aunt Naomi. (pp. 6-7)

The paperback version of *Raney* has passed its 30th printing. Ironically, at the time of the novel's early success, Algonquin Books had a New York agent who was supposed to sell the paperback rights but refused in a letter, stating: "*Raney* will not fit today's fiction market."

Clyde's next novel, *Walking Across Egypt*, sold 34,000 hardback copies and well over 300,000 paperback copies. It was also made into a movie, one of my sister Andrea's favorite films.

Clyde has never been very concerned about sales figures and is reluctant discussing the business side of his craft—although at this point in his career the combined sales (hardback and paper) of his first eight novels exceed one million books. He sees his job as "writing good fiction" and doesn't concern himself with the marketing or deal making. He leads a fairly simple, fulfilling life of writing, teaching, being a dad, composing and playing music, and doing readings. He is a superb, captivating reader—"the best," according to my sister Sally (and I would concur), but he hates all the traveling. And, as his many friends will attest, he has not let his success change his basic personality. He is the same bright, funny, hard working, warm, loyal, engaging person he always was.

Okay, he's not *exactly* the same. When I met Clyde in his bachelor days, his apartment was something out of a Neil Simon play, Early Oscar Madison. The refrigerator lodged nothing more than a few beers and something that, once food, was now a science experiment. His Air Force poncho was the "curtain" he so artistically tacked up over the bedroom window. The bathroom had a bright red, heart-shaped trashcan and a green throw rug with a spider-in-web design. Various holes adorned various lamp shades. A framed dentistry diploma of one Lucy Sherwood, a document Clyde found at a garage sale, hung on the living room wall. The living room table was an old, handle-less suitcase atop a wooden crate.

QUITE A CAREER

Clyde has published numerous articles and reviews, short stories, plays, songs, musicals, and novels. After *Raney* (1985) and *Walking Across Egypt* (1987) came *The Floatplane Notebooks* (1988), *Killer Diller* (1991), *In Memory of Junior* (1992), *Redeye: A Western* (1995), *Where Trouble Sleeps* (1997),

Lunch at the Picadilly (2003), *Solo: My Adventures in the Air* [nonfiction] (2005), and *The Bible Salesman* (2008).

Writing is typically a solitary craft: a process of ideas and elaboration, brainstorming and refining, revising and polishing. It is a process that inevitably involves rejection—sometimes a great deal of rejection. It is a process that, in order to succeed, forces the writer to confront the criticism—to further probe, develop, rework, and polish.

In a 1992 interview, Clyde talked about how he learned to deal with rejection. When he started sending his stories out, he contacted the "big magazines like *Esquire* or *The New Yorker* … and I always got back rejections." The same thing happened when he sought out the "big literary journals like the *The Georgia Review* and *The Virginia Quarterly Review*." It was a "discouraging" time, he admits. "However, I liked writing so I kept sending out my stories. Occasionally, a rejection would offer a helpful comment." When he started submitting his work to the smaller journals, he began to find success.

"I have since learned that most writers get many, many rejections," Clyde once said. "I have also learned that editors' tastes vary greatly, just as some people have tastes in clothes that are different from your own. Be prepared for magazines and publishers to reject what you write. That's just the way it works. Even though I have published five novels, I still get more rejections of my short stories than I get acceptances. After William Faulkner won the Nobel Prize for Literature, he had short stories rejected by magazines."

For the many, many writers who aspire to reach the level of a full-time author like Clyde Edgerton, writing is a process not only of hard work but of dreams. Once upon a time, Clyde Edgerton was like so many who hunger to be writers. He had the dream; he had the desire; he had the talent; he had the work ethic. And he finally realized the dream.

But there was a critical juncture, a particular point in time when he was ready to stop dreaming, to stop working, to stop writing fiction. He didn't. And that has made a significant difference for millions the world over who read and reread his work … and look forward to the next and the next and the next.

REFERENCES

Bell, J. S. (2004). Rejecting rejection. *Right-Writing.com*. Retrieved September 4, 2008, from http://www/right-writing.com/rejection.html

Edgerton, C.. (1985). *Raney, A novel*. Chapel Hill, NC: Algonquin Books of Chapel Hill.

Minah, J. (2003). Understanding rejection slips. *WritersBreak.com.* Retrieved September 4, 2008, from http://www.writersbreak.com/Fiction/articles/article_fiction_rejectionslips.htm.
Scheft, B. (2002). *The ringer.* New York: Harper Collins.
Scheft, B. (2005). *Time won't let me.* New York: HarperCollins.

CHAPTER 19

DEALING
WITH DIALECT DIFFERENCES

Honest Concerns and Practical Approaches

Tom Scheft

Editor's Note: This next article first appeared in the Fall 1995 edition of *Education Issues*, the journal of the University of South Carolina at Spartanburg School of Education, Volume 6, Number 1. It is reprinted with permission. I've made some slight alterations from the original text.

I include it here because it has been an integral part of my "message" to teachers and students about writing and speaking. In terms of this book, a skilled writer should have plenty of dialects in his/her arsenal. And the same goes for all you skilled human beings.

Dialect is such an important concern. An educator's failure to understand and appreciate dialect differences can lead to destructive consequences for some students. Over the years I am simultaneously chilled and saddened by the students who inform me, usually in the middle of a conversation, that they "can't speak." My reply: "Well you seem to be doing a terrific job." Then comes the typical reply: "Well … you know what I mean."

And—of course—I do. And I don't.

This is just the tip of that ol' iceberg.

* * *

Inspiring Student Writers: Strategies and Examples for Teachers
pp. 177–187
Copyright © 2009 by Information Age Publishing

We love to laugh … often at inappropriate things. Asked to define the difference between comedy and tragedy, comedian Mel Brooks explained that when he got a tiny paper cut, that was tragic, but when someone fell down an open manhole cover and died … now *that* was funny. Humor comes from a variety of sources—often those xenophobic, ethnocentric, and racist tendencies that make us all too human. That which is *different* is the stuff of humor, and the way people talk—determined largely by socioeconomic, geographical, and cultural variables—is very dissimilar. A current comedy staple, the rural Southern accent, is used to imply stupidity, lack of intelligence. As one comic has mused: If Einstein had talked with a drawl, proclaiming "A ay-quills e-um say sq-way-ed" ($E = MC^2$), no one would have taken his discovery seriously.

In the midst of an American culture that has a penchant for clashing over that which is different, many schools nationwide have embraced a multicultural curriculum. The premise is quite simple: By learning about diverse cultures, students will have a heightened awareness, leading to a greater appreciation of and respect for cultural diversity. The multicultural curriculum attempts to combat basic stereotypical tendencies and biases by demonstrating that differences don't mean deficiencies. While certain schools are making progress in this area, one area of distinction continues to promote instantaneous assumptions of good and bad, correct and incorrect, proper and improper, standard and substandard. Dialect.

In 1973, I read an article by Jane W. Torrey in Frank Smith's *Psycholinguistics and Reading* that has forever influenced my teaching. Titled "Illiteracy in the Ghetto," the work explored Torrey's concern that dialect differences from standard English were the reason many African Americans had problems in school and even dropped out of school. However, when Torrey researched the *structural* differences between standard dialect and what she termed "Afro-American dialect," and when she studied the research of William Labov and others, she concluded that the minor structural differences were not a problem for African Americans and did not pose difficulties in basic communication and understanding. For example, consider the syntactical and communicative similarities of these two sentences:

My brother he be at Susan house with her three sister.

My brother is at Susan's house with her three sisters.

While the usage differences are apparent, the grammatical structures are almost identical, and the vast majority of readers or listeners would have no trouble agreeing that the meanings are identical.

These next two sentences illustrate the same points:

I don't have any apples.

I ain't got no apples.

No one I know has any problem seeing the meanings as synonymous. And while some might hastily interject, "What about the double negative?"— that construction does not result in miscommunication. No one I've ever met has heard "I ain't got no apples," and then expected a bunch of fruit.

Having established the similarity in English dialect structures, Torrey turns to the *function* of dialects and boldly states:

> My thesis is that the main impact of Afro-American dialect on education has not been its structural differences from standard English, nor its relative intrinsic usefulness as a medium of thought, but its function as a low-status stigma and its association with a rejected culture. The attitudes of teachers toward this dialect and of dialect speakers towards the teachers' language have affected the social relationships of children with the schools in such a way as to make education of many children almost impossible. Black children of rural Southern background have entered the urban schools to find that nearly everything they said was branded as "wrong." In order to be "right" they had to adopt forms that seemed alien even when they were able to learn how to use them. Their own spontaneous products were punished and treated as worthless, including the only language they knew really well. Because of this, they were almost forced to regard themselves and their society as bad, ugly, or even sinful. (Smith, 1973, p. 135)

Most of my students are from the South. I like to ask them how people from other geographic areas have reacted to their speech. Their stories are predictable. In an age in which political correctness has retired a number of stereotypes, the Southern accent immediately conveys stupidity to a vast, *accepting* audience. Moreover, our media bombard us with programming and advertisements that subtly and overtly inculcate us to the maxim that "different is deficient." Multiculturalism has a tough fight against the glitz and glamour of billion dollar industries with proven track records of winning the hearts and minds and bucks of the masses.

But if it's a fight, then let's pass out the ammunition. I offer these salient, yet often misunderstood, points:

1. A dialect is a *variation* of a language (not a separate language) spoken by a group of people who are set apart by geographic area, socioeconomic status, and/or culture.
2. Grammar is customarily defined as syntax (word order) and usage (the customary use of words and phrases).

(a) All dialects are grammatical. They use word order that expresses an idea; their purpose is communication.

(b) Most children comprehend the basic grammatical patterns of language before they begin elementary school.

(c) An important question: If usage is the customary use of words and phrases, *whose custom* are we talking about? Is it a graduate student at M.I.T.; a ranch hand in Amarillo, Texas; a farmer in Durham, North Carolina; a movie executive in Los Angeles; a politician from Brooklyn, New York; a television cooking show host from Baton Rouge, Louisiana?

(d) While different dialects may employ different grammatical structures and usage, all are rule-based, a fact many people are unaware of—preferring in their ignorance to label differences as "errors." What the uneducated critic may view as "carelessness" or linguistic "unsophistication" is neither.

Of course, knowing this information may not be enough. It takes courage to educate people who have been conditioned for a long time. We are exposed to media that push us to consider "who's in and who's out," "what's hot and what's not." There is also historical precedent. Why is tennis scored with the terms "love" and "deuce" and interchangeable numbers like "5" and "15"? Answer: The king wanted a scoring system that the peasants couldn't understand. That kind of logic is still with us.

GOOD INTENTIONS ARE NOT ENOUGH

These misconceptions about dialect in the hands of the best intentioned teacher can cause psychological damage, sometimes serious and prolonged. As Torrey notes, the teacher who tries to "stamp out" a dialect difference, who brands a student's speech as "wrong" or "bad" or "incorrect" or "improper," who disparages a child's spontaneous language not only sends a negative message about the child, but also about the child's family, extended family and community. The impact can be particularly harmful to very young children:

> Children in the lower grades commonly accept a teacher as a kind of substitute mother. Teachers make use of this attitude in motivating and teaching. However, no such mother-child relationship can be established with someone who cannot accept the other person and his ways as legitimate. (Smith, 1973, p. 135)

I have my students read the Shirley Jackson short story, "After you, My Dear Alphonse," to show them how good intentions are easily and quickly subverted by stereotypes and misperceptions, resulting in alienation rather than understanding. I also use the first 10 minutes of the film *Black History: Lost, Stolen or Strayed* (CBS, 1968) to enhance Torrey's message that dangerous psychological consequences result from an ignorance about language use and history.

NOT JUST A BLACK-WHITE ISSUE

While most of my students are African American, many of my Caucasian students talk about the alienation they've experienced with their parents and community members who did not go to college. The family/community "country" dialect is seen as "normal" or "uneducated," while the student's new use of standard English is seen as "educated" or an obvious affront, a put-down. Reactions can be extreme—ranging from a parent's enormous pride in a child's new speech to a deep sense of shame and inferiority.

EXPLAINING LINGUISTIC PLURALITY

In her article, Torrey calls for linguistic plurality—the *adding on* of dialects for use depending upon setting, audience, and purpose. Many know this by the term "code switching." Children as young as 5 and 6 years old understand that we talk differently based on whom we are with, where we are, and what we want. An easy exercise to explain this, which I've used with children and adults, involves putting four categories on the board:

Buddy Talk   School Talk   Home Talk   Job Talk

Take a situation, such as greeting someone. Typical ninth grade students might offer these buddy salutations:

"What's up?" (not necessarily a question to be answered) (There are variations on this theme, such as "Whazzup" or the wonderfully compacted "Zup.")

"Yo." (This greeting is nicely complemented by a Noun of Direct Address, as in "Yo, dude." "Yo, man." "Yo, Fred." "Yo, dawg.")

Words beginning with "H." ("Hi." "Hello." "Hey.")

But how would these ninth graders greet their principal, Mr. Smith? If you're dealing with *real* students, usually a hand flies up from a male student and he responds, "Yo, whazzup, dawg?"—which gets a good laugh. And this *is* how that student (and a few others in class) would greet the principal. But not everybody would, and that is a key point. Different does not mean deficient—which prompts the question: How would you greet the principal in a way you wouldn't greet your friends? That brings on these typical responses:

"Good morning, Mr. Smith."

"How are you doing, Mr. Smith?"

And this leads to the next question: What would be the reaction of some ninth graders if their friends greeted them with "Good morning"? It might be a "What planet are you from?" expression. This lets you talk about *purpose*—wanting to fit in, wanting to be accepted, not wanting to be labeled "weird" or "geeky" or anything negative.

Purpose is a logical transition to the next category, *Job Talk*. If you want a job, how do you greet Ms. Jones, the interviewer? What would Ms. Jones think if she heard: "Yo, Ms. J, dawg, so like, um, how you doin'? Dat job still open?"

Another good example to use is the compliment. How would eleventh graders tell a buddy they liked his/her shirt? Some very acceptable ways to show your approval in the last decade are "fly," "tight," "slammin'," "dope," and "phat."

And how would that work praising your mother's new outfit? "Hey, Mom, you look really phat and tight!" ("Put down that knife, Mom! It's a compliment! Honest!")

And the boss's new threads? "Boss, that suit is dope."

This is not something that's especially new to students, but they need to discuss it in the formality of the classroom, and it needs to be clearly related to our language goals and objectives. Students who deeply resent having to manipulate their speech (because they think it makes them sound "like a sellout" or "white" or whatever) have no trouble admitting they make very conscious decisions about what to wear for a job interview or on a date or to school.

A STRATEGY FOR SELF-AWARENESS

For students to use different dialects, they must

- understand linguistic plurality,
- have a purpose for embracing it, and

- have opportunities to practice dialects in order to feel fluent and comfortable.

One of the best ways to establish purpose is to ask a student: What do you want to be when you grow up? What careers do you want to pursue? If the answers are "doctor," "lawyer," "CEO of Apple Inc.," you've got the student's motivation working for you. But what about the student who wants to be a "famous athlete"? That student still needs to get into college and get through college. Pro careers are relatively short. Will she or he then want to get a broadcasting job? Write his/her memoirs? Hit the lecture circuit? Coach? Do commercials? Make movies? Dialect considerations come into play. Many of the same questions apply to the student who wants to be a "famous rapper."

You may not be able to reach all your students with this logic, because there are successful careers that don't require standard English. In Durham, North Carolina where I teach, you can find a number of students who could say, "I don't need to talk or write like that because I'm gonna inherit my family's farm and make 10 times more money than you'll ever make" ... and, you know, the kid's got a point.

PRACTICING THAT'S FUN

Idea 1: Shouting. A friend of mine who taught 10th graders at a rural Southern school in the 1970s would take his classes out behind the building where there was a forest. He would say something in nonstandard English, and the class would yell the standard equivalent.

He: Your mama don't dance and your daddy don't rock 'n' roll.

They: YOUR MOTHER DOESN'T DANCE AND YOUR FATHER DOESN'T ROCK AND ROLL.

He: You ain't nothin' but a hound dog.

They: YOU AREN'T ANYTHING BUT A HOUND DOG.

The students loved to do this, and pretty soon he was able to manipulate this based on the Premack Principle: If you do a good job with _____ today, I'll put aside some time for shouting tomorrow.

Idea 2: 1-and-1 Basketball Foul Shots. Students love to throw paper balls in trash cans. Divide the class into teams. Set up foul lines and wastebaskets. Give a student a nonstandard English sentence. If he provides the standard equivalent, it's one point and a chance to earn another point by sinking a shot.

Idea 3: Lyric Transcriptions. Students love music, and there is a lot of popular music that incorporates slang and nonstandard dialect. After some preliminary discussion about appropriate content and *some judicious previewing* by the teacher, have students provide translations and transcriptions of some of their favorite songs. There are a variety of appropriate songs for almost any thematic concept a teacher chooses.

When my son was in high school, one of his English teachers used a variation of this assignment. Students had to take the prologue from *Romeo and Juliet* and transcribe it using a different character type and/or accent. My son decided on using a voice from a popular TV show at the time, *The Sopranos*, which featured mobsters from New Jersey. First, here's Shakespeare's original version:

> Two households, both alike in dignity,
> In fair Verona, where we lay our scene,
> From ancient grudge break to new mutiny,
> Where civil blood makes civil hands unclean.
> From forth the fatal loins of these two foes
> A pair of star-cross'd lovers take their life;
> Whole misadventured piteous overthrows
> Do with their death bury their parents' strife.
> The fearful passage of their death-mark'd love,
> And the continuance of their parents' rage,
> Which, but their children's end, nought could remove,
> Is now the two hours' traffic of our stage;
> The which if you with patient ears attend,
> What here shall miss, our toil shall strive to mend.

And now Daniel's adaptation:

> Okay, youse got deese two families
>   with the same amount of dough.
> In fair Brooklyn is where it's going down.
> There's been bad blood forever,
>   and now there's new violence
> With guys gettin' whacked
>   and blood sprayin' all over da place.
> Each family had a kid,
> And you didn't have to be no psychic
>   with an astrology chart to know
>   deese two end up sleepin' with the fishes;
> Cuz of their dumb deaths
> Da families will forgedaboutit; there's gonna be a truce.
> So you got these two suicidal losers,
> And their families' anger would have gone on,
> Except you got these two freakin' stiffs and dat's dat,

Which you can check out for a couple a hours;
If you don' know what I'm saying, you moron,
　　Watch da freakin' play.

Idea 4: Explore the Effectiveness of Different Dialects Through Literature. Demonstrate the power of dialect by reading and studying passages from Ralph Ellison, Mark Twain, Eudora Welty, Richard Wright, Maya Angelou, Clyde Edgerton, and other excellent writers.

TAKING AWAY THE PSYCHOLOGICAL STING

Plenty of parents have been known to waggle a finger at a child and proclaim, "I don't want to hear that kind of incorrect English in this house!" And a parent's rebuke is an effective way to change behavior.

Of course the psychological dimension is quite different when the scolding comes from a parent as opposed to a teacher. However, oftentimes the kid just doesn't get the point. For example, the young child who says "We goed to the store" constructs that verb out of intelligence, not stupidity. It's quite common for young children to logically "invent" constructions after internalizing the basic rules of usage.

I discovered a magic phrase in 1973 that allows one to gently get children to consider language alternatives:

What's another way to say that?

I have used this question with literally hundreds of children from various cultures, regions, socioeconomic backgrounds, and races. A typical exchange might go as follows:

Child: I was playing in the kitchen, and I breaked a dish.
Me: Do you know another way to say that?
Child: I breaked the dish *yesterday*?
Me: I meant do you know another way to say "*breaked*."
Child: You mean, I broke the dish?
Me: Yes. "I broke the dish" is another way to say it.

I have yet to meet a child who couldn't do this. Most often the response is instantaneous. Sometimes prompting is needed. I don't make a big deal out of the standard usage, and I absolutely do not use words like "correct," "good," or "proper." A first grade teacher who employs this strategy may present the concept of standard usage to her students by calling it "the school way" of speaking and writing. She can explain that different practices occur at different places; for example, "the school way" for drinking milk is out of a half-pint carton, while "the home way" is out of a glass or mug.

As children get older, it is important to discuss with them people's xenophobic, ethnocentric, and racist tendencies and how this affects societal standards of language and other customs. But we must go beyond merely pointing out information. Students need appropriate coping strategies, and we must tap into their motivation to embrace linguistic plurality.

Marva Collins, a renowned teacher, tells her students they must learn to communicate in standard English, but she also acknowledges the power of communication in all dialects—especially those of her children. She does more than pay lip service to the concept; she incorporates salient dialect sayings and expressions in her speech.

NOT A DENIAL OF STANDARDS

Some people misunderstand linguistic plurality and describe it as a "denial of standards," an "anything goes" approach to communication. Not true. It is a recognition of *specific* standards based on time and place. It emphasizes the power of the person who commands a fluency of dialects. It is about power and comfort and understanding.

Many teachers *assume* students know they are to communicate using standard dialect on tests and in papers, but teachers need to explain *why* it is their standard and *when* it is expected. That's honest and important.

TRUE STORY

When my son, Daniel, was 1-and-a-half, he had a unique way of asking questions. Instead of pointing at something and saying "What is it?", Daniel would ask, "What it is?"

One day we were grocery shopping, and Daniel was riding in the cart. Behind us pulled up an African American teenager sporting an ornate medallion. My son thrust out a chubby finger toward the young man's jewelry, looked up at him, and said, "What it is?"

Whereupon the young man grabbed my son's hand, shook it, and said with a smile, "What it is, little bro.'" Then, turning to me, he added: "That is one very hip kid you got."

Word up.

REFERENCES

CBS News (Producer). (1968). *Of Black America series: Black history: Lost, stolen or strayed* [Film]. Santa Monica, CA: BFA Educational Media.

Torrey, J. W. (1973). Illiteracy in the ghetto. In F. Smith (Ed.), *Psycholinguistics and reading* (pp. 131-137). New York: Hold, Rinehard and Winston.

ABOUT THE EDITOR

Tom Scheft, an associate professor in the School of Education at North Carolina Central University, teaches educational psychology and instructional planning ("a great course that combines psycholinguistics, lesson planning, classroom management, multiculturalism, and other important concerns"). Scheft has been at NCCU "a frighteningly long time" (since 1978). He is a recipient of the NCCU Teaching Excellence Award.

When he's not teaching, a favorite thing to do is "bash away on the drums." He is a member of "the most famous group you never heard of"—The Rising Storm, a rock group that formed in high school and is featured in Ritchie Unterberger's *Unknown Legends of Rock 'n' Roll*. (Honest.) "We still get together, sometimes record, sometimes play live, and we've even played in Europe," he says. "My son, Daniel, calls it 'geezer rock' and likes to say, 'Gee, Dad, the people I listen to went platinum. I hear the Storm just went coal.'"